The Cambridge Manuals of Science and Literature

PLATO
MORAL AND POLITICAL IDEALS

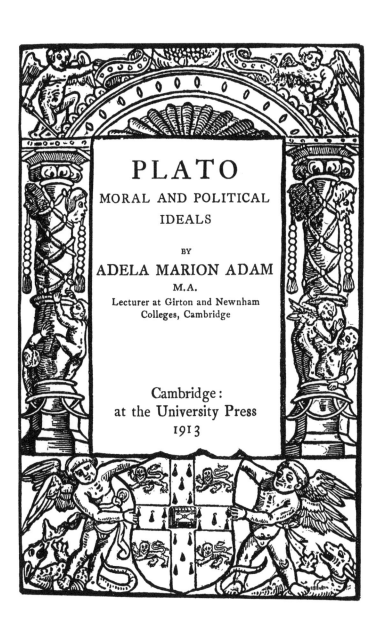

PLATO

MORAL AND POLITICAL IDEALS

BY

ADELA MARION ADAM

M.A.

Lecturer at Girton and Newnham
Colleges, Cambridge

Cambridge:
at the University Press
1913

CAMBRIDGE UNIVERSITY PRESS
Cambridge, New York, Melbourne, Madrid, Cape Town,
Singapore, São Paulo, Delhi, Tokyo, Mexico City

Cambridge University Press
The Edinburgh Building, Cambridge CB2 8RU, UK

Published in the United States of America by
Cambridge University Press, New York

www.cambridge.org
Information on this title: www.cambridge.org/9781107401860

© Cambridge University Press 1913

First published 1913
First paperback edition 2011

A catalogue record for this publication is available from the British Library

ISBN 978-1-107-40186-0 Paperback

Cambridge University Press has no responsibility for the persistence or
accuracy of URLs for external or third-party internet websites referred to in
this publication, and does not guarantee that any content on such websites is,
or will remain, accurate or appropriate.

*With the exception of the coat of arms
at the foot, the design on the title page is a
reproduction of one used by the earliest known
Cambridge printer, John Siberch, 1521*

PREFACE

WHEN the Editor invited me to contribute this volume to the *Cambridge Manuals of Science and Literature*, he wrote that he wished for "a clear account, intelligible to the plain man, of what Plato did in the moral and political sphere." Recently the difficulty of deciding what was Plato's teaching in any part of his philosophy has greatly increased. The publication in 1911 of Professor A. E. Taylor's *Varia Socratica, First Series*, and of Professor J. Burnet's Introduction to his edition of the *Phaedo* has obliged all students of Plato to reconsider their position. These two writers hold, to put it briefly, that neither Xenophon nor Aristotle knew much about Socrates, except what they learnt through Plato and his school, and that therefore the works of Plato are practically the only source of our knowledge of Socrates. Professor Taylor, moreover, considers that Aristophanes, in his play, *The Clouds*, produced when Plato was a boy of four, draws a caricature of Socrates, which is confirmed, even in details, by the picture of him found in the Platonic writings ; and Professor Burnet thinks that Plato's original opinions are only to be found in those dialogues, generally attributed to his later period, in which he criticises doctrines upheld in other works, commonly supposed to be of earlier date.

If this is the case, it would be exceedingly difficult to write anything about the moral and political teaching of Plato, and it may be that this book should have an *erratum* slip attached to it, stating that the title ought to be *Socrates : Moral and Political Ideals*. But I am not yet prepared to reduce Plato's achievement to the glory of relegating Boswell to the second place among biographers. Xenophon must have been an even more inept person than he is usually considered, if he carefully sifted out and rejected all the most interesting characteristics of Socrates that appear in Plato, in order to compile his *Memorabilia*. It may readily be admitted that the early dialogues of Plato, such as the *Charmides* and the *Laches*, give a much more attractive and credible account of the historical Socrates than Xenophon's somewhat lifeless portraiture. But the main obstacle to adopting the view of Professor Taylor and Professor Burnet seems to be the difficulty of reconciling the content of these and other " Socratic " dialogues with that of the *Symposium*, *Phaedrus*, *Republic*, and so forth.

Mr F. M. Cornford, who also feels this difficulty,[1] meets it by supposing that Plato, when he wrote

[1] In *From Religion to Philosophy*, pp. 242, 247 ff.

the early dialogues, was not fully conversant with the teaching of Socrates, and that it was not until he had become acquainted with Pythagoreans in Sicily and Greece, after the death of his master, that he learnt to appreciate his mystical side. I prefer, until further evidence is produced, to hold by the older view, that the vastly increased range of thought in Plato's greater works represents the development of his own mental powers. I have tried to trace this development, as regards one department of philosophy, and am left with the conviction that Plato could not have transformed the Socrates of the *Crito* into Socrates, who in the *Republic* is the spectator of all time and all existence, merely by becoming, through the good offices of a group of friends, more familiar with the doctrine of a teacher (whom he, as a full-grown young man, knew and loved personally), many years after that teacher's death.

In the earlier chapters I have made much use of MS. notes for lectures by my husband. If any former pupils of Dr Henry Jackson read this book, they will recognise how great is my debt to him.

A. M. A.

CAMBRIDGE, *March* 1913.

CONTENTS

PLATO
MORAL AND POLITICAL IDEALS

CHAPTER I

GREEK ETHICS AND POLITICS BEFORE SOCRATES

In attempting to introduce a reader to any part of
Plato's thought, the first problem that presents
itself is the choice of a starting-point. The ethics
of Plato, like all Greek ethics, are inextricably
bound up with his politics, and neither the one nor
the other can be understood without a study of his
metaphysics or, what comes to the same thing, his
theology. Further, Plato himself does not suddenly
sweep into our ken in the fourth century B.C. as
a new and brilliant planet. Though his light far
outshines that of all his fellow-countrymen who
preceded him as philosophical and religious teachers,
yet every one of these has contributed something
to his splendour, and if we seek to find out at
what Plato was aiming, we must learn upon what
substratum of earlier and contemporary notions
his mind was at work. Above all, we must
consider his relationship to his beloved master

Socrates, that master whom he described as " the best of the men of his time whom we knew, yea and the wisest and most just."

The term " ethics," in Greek ἠθικά, in Latin *moralia*, means by derivation " what appertains to human character (ἦθος)." The study of ethics, ἡ ἠθική, is therefore the study of everything which has a bearing on human character. Now character is assumed by Plato, and by Aristotle after him, to depend largely on conduct. " In infancy," says Plato, " more than at any other time the formation of the whole character depends on habit," and, similarly, Aristotle enunciates as a general law the principle that virtuous or vicious moral states are the result of habitual virtuous or vicious actions. Aristotle states with great precision at the opening of his *Ethics*, that every systematic action has some end in view. It is therefore found that human character and conduct (which latter, as we have just seen, was recognised as a factor of the highest importance in character) are best studied with reference to what is called the chief good or end of man and everything relating to that end.

In our day, the word ethics is used of the study which relates to the end of man considered as a private individual, but among the Greeks, down to the time of Aristotle, man was viewed less as an individual than as a citizen. We look upon the individual as the unit, the State as an aggregate of units. Plato or Aristotle would call the State the unit, the individual merely a fraction. From this point of view ethics cannot be separated from politics. For instance, Plato's *Republic*, or " State," though it purports to be a political treatise, is at least as much a work on ethics as on politics. Aristotle, on the other hand, wrote, perhaps some fifteen or twenty years after Plato's death, two books, one called *Ethics*, the other *Politics*, but, as Professor Burnet says, he " excuses himself for appearing to separate " the two subjects. His *Ethics* is, as it were, the first instalment of his work on politics. Similarly, in common Greek parlance, the rule of morality for the individual is equivalent to the law of the State ; " what is established by law " (τὸ νόμιμον) and " what is right " (τὸ δίκαιον) are interchangeable phrases.

In the earlier times of Greek thought little or no trace is to be found of scientific ethico-political studies. Hesiod, Theognis and the lyric poets loved to moralise, but their reflections are sporadic, not combined into any systematic whole. One principle that frequently emerges is the duty of doing good to friends and harm to foes. Hesiod (*Works and Days*, 709 ff.) gives us possibly the earliest statement in Greek literature of this precept. " If thy comrade is the first to do thee an unkind-

ness either in word or in deed, forget not to requite
him two-fold; howbeit, if he would lead thee again
into friendship, and is willing to make restitution,
do not say him nay." We may note in passing
the extreme severity of the maxim as thus presented; two eyes, two teeth are to be exacted for
one by him who would do justly. Other doctrines
of much significance were embodied in short sayings,
attributed now to one, now to another of the per-
sonages known as the Seven Wise Men, and the most
celebrated of these aphorisms, " Know thyself " and
" Nothing in excess," were, as we learn from Plato
and others, kept continually before the mind of
the Hellenic world through being inscribed on the
temple of Apollo at Delphi. These two maxims
respectively developed into the important doctrines
of the necessity of self-knowledge, and of virtue
considered as a mean between two opposite extremes of vice. But the wisdom of the Wise Men
did not attain to a full-grown ethical system, and
before the time of Socrates there were but few
thinkers who tried to make their ethics part and
parcel of their philosophy in general. Of these
few the most important are Pythagoras (or rather
the Pythagorean school), Heraclitus, and possibly
Democritus.

Aristotle and his followers tell us that Pythagoras (*flor. circ.* 530 B.C.) reduced the various

virtues to numbers. Justice, for example, was a square number, because justice (as in the ordinary Greek view) was looked on as a matter of equal give-and-take symbolised by the multiplication of a number into itself. Further, Pythagoras is said to have held that virtue is a harmony, friendship a harmonious equality, and so on. The importance of this rudimentary attempt at an ethical system lies in the effort to find a place for ethics inside Pythagoreanism in general. He aimed at bringing ethics into line with his first principle, which was that all is number. What he meant by this *dictum* we need not here inquire. The point to notice is the method, which in this case is more valuable than the result.

Heraclitus (*flor. circ.* 500 B.C.), employing the same method, reached more striking results. According to him, the only thing that really exists is change—change, ceaseless and universal. To this change he gave different names, corresponding to the aspect in which it may be viewed. Sometimes he called it Fire (which is, as it were, change materialised), sometimes Justice, or again Fate, Harmony, the Universal Word or Reason, which was held to be synonymous with God, a self-conscious principle pervading all that is, at once the creator and controller of the universe. In our own day a new impulse has been given to the

Heraclitean view of the world, through M. Bergson's doctrine that life and reality consist in ceaseless change and movement. To Heraclitus this all-pervading principle is in and around us ; we inhale it with our breath, and through it the discord of life is turned into music, "for," says Heraclitus, anticipating Keats, "the unheard harmony is better than the heard."

How does Heraclitus bring ethics into connexion with his philosophic principle ? In one of his fragmentary sayings, preserved to us by quotations in later authors, he says, "Wherefore we must follow the Universal, but although Reason is Universal, most men live as if they had a private wisdom of their own." That is to say, most men err in not seeing that their end or chief good consists in subordinating themselves to the spirit that pervades all nature. "An overweening temper must be extinguished more than a conflagration." Law and due measure must be sought, for "the ever-living fire is quenched and rekindled in due measure," and "all human laws are fed by the one divine law," so that "the people must fight for the law as for their town wall." All this points forward to the view that we shall presently find enunciated with emphasis by Plato, that the end for mankind is assimilation to God, as far as is possible for a human being.

Democritus (*flor. circ.* 420 B.C.) upheld the doctrine of an inexorable natural and materialistic law. Aristotle tells us that he looked upon the universe as consisting of a mass of atoms moving eternally in a void. From their collisions arises the variety of existing things. Man's duty and chief good is to cultivate a calm unruffled mind, seeing that he is a thing of nought in the grip of the eternal mechanism.

About the time of Democritus there arose in various parts of Greece a body, not so much of original thinkers like the three philosophers at whose opinions we have just been glancing and others who left ethics and politics on one side, as of professional teachers, who gave instruction in all manner of subjects for pecuniary reward. These men bore the general name of sophists. They travelled about from place to place, and the leaders among them gained great reputations and large fortunes into the bargain. Some taught astronomy, others mathematics, music, and other subjects too numerous to mention, but the majority professed to teach social and civic excellence or ἀρετή—the art of living well (τὸ εὖ ζῆν). The ministrations of the sophists were provided in response to the growing demand on the part of Greek, especially Athenian, youth for such an education as would qualify them for civic life.

Now if excellence had to be *taught*, it was necessary that the current vague and inconsistent notions about the terms " virtue," " goodness," " justice," and so forth should be systematised and reconciled ; accordingly clearer and better arranged views on all questions of ethics were sought for. The sophists, for the most part, were content to teach the morality of the day, without investigating its claims to validity, and therefore they failed to satisfy the needs of the more enquiring spirits among their contemporaries. Hence the time was ripe for the introduction of a new method into philosophy, and Socrates was the man who, by inventing one, revolutionised the course of what the last two paragraphs in Aristotle's *Ethics* call " the philosophy that deals with things human," that is to say, the investigation of moral and political ideas.

CHAPTER II

THE MORAL AND POLITICAL TEACHING OF
SOCRATES

PLATO puts into the mouth of Socrates, when on trial for his life before the Athenian people, on the charge of corrupting the youth of the city, the following words : " I do nothing but go to and fro, endeavouring to persuade you all, both young and old, not to care about the body or riches, but first and foremost about the soul—how to make the soul as good as possible. I tell you that virtue is not the child of riches, but riches of virtue ; and so with every other good that men possess, alike in private and in public life."

We may dispute for ever how far the famous version of Socrates' defence, given by Plato in his *Apology of Socrates*, represents what Socrates actually said at his trial, but there can be little doubt that the *Apology* has preserved for us the spirit, if not the letter, of the defendant's speech. Socrates believed that he had a divine mission to redeem Athens. He was profoundly convinced that there was something much amiss with the whole body politic of his native city, and, like a

good physician, he first endeavoured to discover
the cause of the disease. Looking round him he
seemed to see everywhere that ignorance produced bad results. If right action was to be found
at all, it was only in the sphere of the mechanical
or professional arts, where correct knowledge leads
to correct execution. A man cannot be a good
carpenter without a knowledge of carpentry, a
good shoemaker without a knowledge of shoe-
making, a good doctor without a knowledge of
medicine, a good musician without a knowledge
of music, or, to take an instance which Socrates
would be very likely to use if he were alive now,
a good airman without a knowledge of motor-
engines. Accordingly, if ignorance is the cause
of bad, and knowledge the cause of good lyre-
playing, why should not ignorance also be the
cause of faulty conduct in the individual and the
State ? And in that case is it not plain that the
true remedy is to remove the ignorance and implant knowledge of man's duty ?

Now Socrates was aware that in his own case he
had only to know what he ought to do in order to
do it. His will never rebelled against his judgment, and he maintained that the same harmony
of understanding and action held good for all men,
if only they possessed a sufficiently clear and firmly-
grasped view as to the nature of goodness. For

in proportion to the insight gained into virtue,
the conviction would grow that man's highest
welfare is achieved by virtuous action, and that
therefore it is truly to his interest to eschew evil
and follow good. Nothing but mental blindness
causes anyone to choose an ignoble or vicious life ;
if we could see far enough, we should feel no in-
ducement to fall away from the path of virtue.
Hence Socrates defined virtue as identical with
knowledge, and single virtues he looked on as
varieties of knowledge. Thus the brave man is
one who *knows* what is or is not terrible, the pious
man one who knows what is due from mankind
to the gods, and so forth.

The maxim that virtue is knowledge is the corner-
stone of Socratic teaching, and the paradox, sharp
as it appears to us at first sight, loses much of
its strangeness when we realise that to Socrates
knowledge meant something very different from
a mere storing-up of ascertained facts in the mind
or in note-books. " The truth is that knowledge,
as understood by Socrates, has the closest possible
relation to the character. It is a certain over-
mastering principle or power that lays hold primarily
indeed of the intellect, but through the intellect
of the entire personality, moulding and disciplining
the will and the emotions into absolute unison
with itself, a principle from which courage, tem-

perance, justice and every other virtue inevitably flow." [1] From this point of view the identification of virtue with knowledge becomes an expression of faith in the goodness of human nature, and in the possibility of guiding every individual in the right way. Once grant that moral evil may be cured by pointing out the road to moral good, and all vices that at present disfigure mankind singly and collectively will vanish and be no more seen.

When Socrates had satisfied himself that the disease under which his city was labouring was lack of knowledge, he set about the cure, endeavouring to impart knowledge to the Athenians. Xenophon, who wrote a book of reminiscences of Socrates, called the *Memorabilia,* tells us that his first step was to delimit the province of knowledge. He set aside the whole of natural science, because he believed that man's efforts could not attain to knowledge in that sphere. In the *Memorabilia* (I.1) reasons are given why Socrates came to this conclusion, namely, the inconsistency of philosophers in their attempts to explain the phenomena of nature, and the fact that man is powerless to produce physical forces such as winds, water and seasons. " If," he argued, " those who know human arts can make use of them, similarly those who know divine things ought to be able to make

[1] Adam, *Religious Teachers of Greece,* p. 329.

use of them, but they cannot, and therefore we infer that such things pass man's understanding." Further, he declared everything relating to the ultimate issue of human action, all prognostications as to the success or failure of an enterprise, to lie beyond the scope of human inquiry, being reserved by the gods for themselves. If we would fain know these things we must apply to the oracles ; μαντική, or the art of inspired divination, is the appointed vehicle of such information. In effect Socrates cuts the sum total of things into two. Over one part he sets reason, and assigns that province to man as the proper object of his study. The other part, consisting, on the one hand, of natural phenomena, and, on the other, of insight into future events, he pronounces to be unknowable to man, except in so far as the gods vouchsafe us a partial knowledge through the instrumentality of seers. We shall find that in Plato the art of divination is dethroned, and the dominion of reason is extended to the whole world, so that thereby religion becomes subordinated to philosophy.

Cicero says that Socrates was the first to call down philosophy from heaven to earth, and he is right in the sense that, according to Socrates, human beings should confine their attention exclusively to the study of human virtue. His duty, therefore, was to reform Athens by becoming an ethical teacher. In this self-imposed mission he started by endeavouring to clear away the rubbish of false persuasion of knowledge, which clogged, as it seemed to him, the way for the entry of true doctrine into men's minds. He would button-hole men in the streets, and after extracting from them some opinion given with cheerful confidence, would convict them of ignorance by demonstrating the inconsistency and irrationality of their utterances. His own attitude was habitually that of the ignorant man asking for information; and the term "Socratic irony" is used to describe this self-depreciation. His victims were not unnaturally apt to get angry. If this happened they would leave him and go to swell the gradually-increasing mass of hostility that in the end burst upon him, causing his condemnation and death. On the other hand, if they felt humbled and penitent, feeling, as Alcibiades says of himself in Plato's *Symposium*, that they could not go on living as before, neglecting their true selves, while taking it upon them to manage the concerns of the Athenians;—if they received the ministrations of Socrates in this way, then he would proceed to give them some positive instruction.

His method in this respect, as in the preliminary clearing and cleansing process, was original, but it determined the course of all succeeding ethical philosophy. Aristotle tells us that to Socrates may justly be ascribed the first introduction of inductive reasoning and definition. " Both these things," he adds, " deal with the foundation of knowledge." Socrates would choose instances—almost always from every-day life—of persons or actions to which we apply some particular predicate denoting a moral quality, and after eliminating all that seemed unessential, to attempt a definition of the quality in question. In this way he was led to define virtue as knowledge, and if asked, " knowledge of what ? " he would reply, " knowledge of the good," or, in other words, what is *useful* ($\dot{\omega}\phi\acute{\epsilon}\lambda\iota\mu o\nu$) for the soul's health.

We see, then, that Socrates was a thorough-going rationalist as regards the ordering of men's personal lives. His attitude towards the guidance of the community is entirely in accordance with this fundamental principle of his teaching, and may be summed up in the words, " They only shall rule who know." In Athens, even more than in our own country at the present day, every man thought he knew about politics without the necessity of any preliminary apprenticeship. Moreover, inasmuch as every freeborn Athenian citizen was as such eligible to office, it is plain that ignorance in power might be more instantly disastrous than with us, for whom the filtering process of representation, however crude it may be, does at least impose some check on the impetuous folly of unthinking rulers. Socrates was right in his diatribes against the absurdity of requiring every artist and handicraftsman to have skill, while winking at ignorance in the greatest of all arts, the art of politics, where the stake is far higher than in any other. This Socratic demand for knowledge in politics has been called by Nohle, in his clear-sighted monograph, *Die Staatslehre Platos*, " das technische Prinzip," the recognition of the liability of politicians, like the rest of the world, to come to grief if they neglect to learn their lessons. We shall see presently that the principle is the bed-rock of Plato's ideal State.

According to Xenophon, Socrates himself was not fully conscious of the antagonism between his principle and the spirit of Athenian democracy. He thought something might yet be made of the Athens of his day, and, with what Nohle calls " a certain naïve optimism," contemplated the possibility that a few leading men, equipped with superior insight, would be able to persuade the mass of the citizens that every one desires to walk uprightly, if some one will only show him how. Accordingly, Socrates encouraged his friend Charmides to enter political life, on the ground that no one ought to withhold himself from the service of his country who has,

like Charmides, gifts which will enable him to en-
hance her greatness. His own abstention from
political life he justifies from purely political motives.
Asked on one occasion how he could expect to make
others statesmen, if he himself, though competent,
took no part in public affairs, he replied (Xen.
Mem. I. 6. 15): "Should I be doing more for
politics if I merely practised as a politician than
by taking care that as many people as possible
should be qualified to be politicians?" His
function was to instil a worthy tradition into statesmen, not himself to be an administrator.

In his aspirations after reform, Socrates showed
a curious blend of old-fashioned ideas, combined
with the latest ways of thinking. The Athens for
which he longed was the Athens of the Persian
wars and some thirty years or so after them, the
Athens which lasted until his own early manhood.
He wished to see his fellow-citizens, like the "men
of Marathon," upright and patriotic, preferring
their country's good to their own immediate interest. In all this he was a *laudator temporis acti*
of the most approved pattern, but he desired to
make use of the new method in order to resuscitate
the old morality. His "men of Marathon" would
have scouted the notion that virtue could be taught ;
virtue to them was a matter of instinct and piety
and holding fast to ancestral tradition. It was

B

from those arch-innovators, the sophists, that
Socrates borrowed his principle that teaching
could produce excellence in a statesman, but he
demanded teaching for the sake of establishing
the old type of excellence on a firmer basis, not,
as with many of the sophists' pupils, with a view
to escaping from the tiresome restrictions of an
antiquated moral ideal.

To Socrates it seemed essential that a government, besides being founded on knowledge of
virtue, should also be supreme, whether the authority be law, or the word of an absolute ruler.
Both in theory and in practice he upheld unflinch-
ing obedience to the laws. We know that on two
occasions he risked his life in order to prevent
illegal violence being done to fellow-citizens, and,
after his own condemnation, he rejected Crito's
entreaties that he would fly from prison. The
law had pronounced sentence of death upon him,
and that was for him enough. Xenophon reports
that he defined justice as identical with the law
of the State (τὸ νόμιμον). This definition is interesting not only in its bearing on Socrates' actions,
but because it represents the standpoint of Greek
thought before the time sometimes called " the
Age of Illumination," when the sophists began
to turn the search-light of criticism on to the traditional morality. Socrates, like Hobbes, asserted

the uncompromising authority and irresponsibility of the ruling power; Nohle points out that both these champions of absolute rule arose in periods when the State was passing through an upheaval, in England during the time of the Puritan Revolution, in Athens when the Peloponnesian war and the new doctrines of the sophists had shaken the foundations of society.

Though the governing authority should be supreme, it must seek the good of its subjects exclusively. There must be no exploitation of offices in the interests of the rulers. As we saw that reason was to be supreme in its own domain, but was not suffered by Socrates to trespass into the area where divination bore sway, so the principle of absolutism is limited by the duty of the governor to be a good shepherd to his flock. We may end this chapter with the words we placed at its head. "How to make the soul as good as possible"—this should be the one and only object of all mankind. Those who are best fitted to know where goodness lies, as rulers or guides must point the way to the rest, who in their turn must faithfully fulfil the behests laid upon them. Thus, and thus only, will the welfare of the individual and the State be attained.

CHAPTER III

PLATO AS A PUPIL OF SOCRATES

PLATO came of an aristocratic house, and his early years were passed in a time which gave little encouragement to a young man of such an origin, himself endowed in surpassing measure with powers of imagination and thought, to turn to the work of piloting his country through the difficult waters of faction and external warfare. The seventh of the so-called " Letters of Plato " tells us that he had intended in his youth to enter public life so soon as he should become his own master, but adds that the revolutionary troubles at Athens under the Thirty, and the shock given to him a few years later, in 399, by the condemnation of Socrates, led him to abandon his purpose. Though the letter is of doubtful authenticity, it gives, all the same, a reasonable account of Plato's motive for abstention from practical politics, and the underlying tradition is likely enough to have been sound. His instincts would have led him naturally away from the noisy democratic party, but on the other hand the cruelty and rapacity of the oligarchs, of whom one of the foremost figures was his mother's

cousin, Critias, repelled him, and he found himself
a homeless wanderer, so far as party politics were
concerned. Several years before the excesses of
the Thirty had stirred in him a feeling of aversion
to the political ways of his own class, the Athenian
disasters in Sicily showed, as Zeller has pointed
out, the terrible punishment which befel the mistakes of unrestrained democracy. It is small
wonder that a youth of generous temperament
and gigantic intellect should have taken refuge in
philosophy.

His education had been, to start with, of the
ordinary kind, with music, poetry and physical
exercises as the staple. At an early time—in
Aristotle's words, ἐκ νέου—he had come into contact with Cratylus, a successor of Heraclitus, and
drunk deep from this source of Heraclitean
doctrine, with results of the first importance for
his later development. When he was aged twenty
there came the greatest event of his life, his meet-
ing with Socrates. Unfortunately no external testi-
mony exists as to the relations between Socrates
and the most distinguished of his disciples, except
a few stories found in the biographies of Plato
written several centuries after his death. These
stories are, if not happy survivals of fact, alluring
in their suggestion of what might have been.
When we are told that one night Socrates dreamt

that a wingless swan perched on him and presently grew wings and flew away with a sweet cry, and that the next day when he met the young Plato for the first time, introduced by his father, he recognised in him the swan of his dream, we should like to believe that the older man grasped at first sight the great qualities of his new friend, even to the point of perceiving how the pupil would rise to intellectual heights beyond the range of the master's thought.

And again, when we read how Plato, after he had begun to seek the company of Socrates, made a bonfire of all the poems, which up to that time it had apparently given him much pleasure to write, summoning in a last hexameter the god Hephaestus to come to his aid, we feel that there must be a germ of truth in a tale which signifies so much devotion to an austere master on the part of a disciple, whose poetical and dramatic imagination would always out, notwithstanding his constant warnings to his readers against the seductions of creative art.

Plato only mentions himself three times in the whole course of his works, and that in an entirely unobtrusive manner. But the picture of Socrates among his followers, which emerges from the Platonic writings, brings vividly before us the kind of intercourse that Plato himself must have experienced and relished as much as any member of the circle. Into the mouth of Alcibiades and Phaedo, of his own brothers Glauco and Adimantus, Plato puts the expression of his deep affection for Socrates ; through Simmias and Cebes he shows the effect of the Socratic stimulus on keen intellects ; when Thrasymachus blusters, or the unhappy Polus ties himself up in argumentative knots, we are sure that in many such scenes the writer has watched with a discriminating eye the master's handling of all sorts and conditions of men, and made use of the experience thereby gained to give life to the exposition of further developments made by himself on the teaching he had received.

After the death of Socrates, Plato had no more thought of political life at Athens. For some twelve years he was hardly in the city at all. He spent some time at Megara with the Socratic philosopher, Euclides,[1] and then embarked upon extraordinarily extensive travels, first to Egypt and Cyrene in North Africa, and then to southern Italy and Sicily. It seems that his return to Athens was made after hazardous adventures. In Sicily he had given offence to Dionysius I., tyrant of Syracuse, and in consequence he found himself

---

[1] This sojourn has been doubted by Lutoslawski, but he does not seem to make out a good case.

turned out and put up for sale as a slave on the island of Aegina. There he was rescued, as the story goes, by a wealthy acquaintance from Cyrene. This man, happening to be at Aegina, paid the price for Plato's ransom, and used the subscription, which had been raised by friends at Athens to compensate him, as a fund to buy a house and garden for Plato, close to the gymnasium and grounds called the Academy. The latter part of the tale, as M. Huit remarks, does not agree very well with the tradition and probability that Plato was himself a man of means. However he may have come by this house, the fact remains that Plato, about the year 387, settled in it for the rest of his life and, by combining the accommodation given by his private quarters and the neighbouring gymnasium, established the school whose name has been ever afterwards associated with university education in all lands.

Here the Socratic plan of instruction by means of walks and talks was continued. The master, in the midst of a group of pupils, would help them to thresh out difficulties ; we hear of many students of distinction, and two women are said to have been among those who attended the school ; this circumstance, if true, must have startled the conventional world at Athens, though it would have been thoroughly in accord with Plato's principles.

This life of teaching and writing (Plato's works are thought by some to have been intended for use as text-books in the school) went on apparently without break, except for two more visits to Sicily, for about forty years, until 347, when it is said that death came to him suddenly at the age of eighty, while attending a wedding-feast.

The influence of Socrates remained with him to the last, though he ranged over fields of thought which his master, if we may trust Xenophon, had never approached, and though the figure of Socrates as an interlocutor disappears from those dialogues which are now generally considered for various reasons to belong to the latest period of Plato's life. Zeller and Gomperz point out that the effect of the death of Socrates upon Plato is shown in the embittered judgment which he passes upon Athenian statesmen, especially in the *Gorgias*. In the opinion of Gomperz, Plato's anger had been kindled afresh by the appearance of a political pamphlet decrying Socrates and justifying his condemnation. Whether this be so, or whether, with W. H. Thompson, we think that Plato's return to his native land was the cause of a revival of resentment in him, there is a sharpness of tone in certain passages that indicates wrath against Athenian statesmen, whose policy had brought about a state of affairs in which such a catastrophe as the execution of Socrates could take place. For example, in *Gorg.* 515 E he accuses Pericles of having made the Athenians idle, cowardly, talkative, and money-grubbing because he first introduced payment for jurymen; in 521 D, speaking in the name of Socrates, he says: "I think that there is hardly an Athenian besides myself, not to call myself the only one, who exercises the true art of politics; I alone of those now alive am a politician." The *Gorgias* has been well called the *Apologia Platonis*, that is to say, Plato's defence of himself for abstaining from political life.[1] Such abstention is part of his faithful following in the footsteps of his master. We shall see presently how the shadow of the trial and death of Socrates caused him not only to despair of his country as it was then constituted, but to call forth the vision of an upward road leading, if men would only cleave to it, to a city set in heaven.

[1] Mr Zimmern, in *The Greek Commonwealth,* p. 154, following the Finnish writer, Sundwall, says that both in the fifth and fourth centuries many members of well-to-do families held office in the State and "showed not the least inclination to be 'driven out of public life.' . . . It is clear that few Athenians followed Plato in despairing of the Republic and retiring into private life to wait for more Utopian times."

CHAPTER IV

AT the beginning of Chapter II we said that the *Apology* represented the spirit of what Socrates said at his trial. This is beyond question true, so far as any statement can be beyond question, which rests entirely on internal probability. At the same time Plato's personality colours the speech. We can only conjecture the date whether of this or of any other Platonic work, but in all likelihood the *Apology*, *Crito*, *Euthyphro*, *Laches* and *Charmides*, which we shall consider in this and the following chapter, all come early in the list. There is no sign-post to guide us in deciding the place of any given dialogue except the nature of the style and subject, with occasionally the marking of an upper limit of time by mention of a historical event. Divergencies of opinion have been astonishingly great ; for instance, the *Phaedrus* has been called the earliest dialogue, and also placed among the latest, whereas most critics would assign it (and with good reason) to a middle period. On the whole, however, there is a fairly general agreement as to what constitutes the early or " Socratic " group of dialogues, written while Plato, as a thinker, remained in the position of Socrates, or advanced not far beyond it. All those mentioned above belong to this class, together with the *Lysis* and *Lesser Hippias* and some others whose authenticity is more doubtful. Gomperz puts the *Euthyphro* and *Crito* a good deal later, on somewhat slender grounds. All the Socratic dialogues are on a comparatively small scale, and much less elaborate than those which we shall count as belonging to the next group. Each one of them follows the Socratic method of induction, and harps, with variations, upon the theme that virtue is knowledge. Special Platonic features, such as the introduction of myths to drive home the lessons taught, emphatic assertions of belief in immortality, and, above all, the characteristic doctrine known as the Theory of Ideas are entirely absent. Further, they all agree in having a clear and flowing style, easy to read and far less complicated than is usually the case with the larger works.

In the *Apology* Plato sees more clearly than the Socrates of Xenophon that there is a gulf between the Athenian state and the realisation of Socratic principles. We saw above, p. 16, that Socrates thought that the one thing needful was the guidance of a few great men who would be able to train a docile people in the way it should go. But the *Apology* shows a dissatisfaction with the condition of the State much greater than we find in any non-Platonic utterances of Socrates. The *Memorabilia* of Xenophon do not indicate that Socrates met with violent opposition in his ordinary conversations ; the *Apology* (23 E) says that he became the object of hatred and calumny, so that the formal accusation was only the outcome of a gathering storm of resentment on the part of various classes whom his cross-examination had goaded to fury, poets, statesmen and craftsmen. Such resistance was not compatible with the cheerful expectation of reforming Athens which the Xenophontic Socrates displays ; his mind indeed seems little troubled with fears lest his views should be unacceptable. We can hardly avoid attributing to Plato the despair manifested by Socrates in the *Apology* of inducing the Athenians at large to listen to him. Doubtless Plato has allowed the event of the trial to direct his backward glance over Socrates' former life. He saw that Athens would have none of his master, and brought this antagonism into a prominence greater than Socrates is likely to have given it in his actual speech.

Moreover, the Socrates of the *Apology* says (31 D) : " You know well that if I had long ago tried to engage in politics, I should long ago have perished without doing either you or myself any good," and a little further on : " there is no man who shall be saved if he offers a genuine opposition either to you or to any other democracy, hindering many unjust and unlawful acts from taking place in the city, but he who would really fight in defence of justice must, if he is to remain unscathed even for a short time, live as a private and not as a public man." This acerbity does not agree at all with the passage from the *Memorabilia* (I. 6. 15) quoted above, p. 17, where Socrates alleged as his sole motive for a non-political life his opinion that he spent his time to better purpose in qualifying others to be statesmen. How could he without warning have urged his friend Charmides to enter the service of the State, if he thought he was sending him to instant destruction ? No, the Socrates who declared in the *Apology* (32 E) that neither he nor anybody else would have reached the age of seventy if he had been in public life and had furthered the cause of justice on every occasion as a good man should, making this his first rule, was a different person from the Socrates who, in Xenophon, gave no hint of danger to would-be politicians of a virtuous sort, but was merely concerned to exhort them to fit themselves for their high office.

As we have seen, Plato's connexion with Critias

and other leading politicians must have shown
him the inner working of the political machine,
and convinced him of its unsound condition. His
disenchantment may have led him to tinge the
words of Socrates with a darker hue than that
which rightly belonged to them. The unjust
judgement convinced him that the impulsive and
undiscerning democracy of Athens was no instrument for carrying out Socratic ideas. To see the
most pious and inspiring teacher in the country
condemned for impiety and corrupting the youth
of the nation, was enough to drive away from Plato's
mind all hope of reform in the State as it was, and
to make him meditate on an ideal city where such
deeds should be impossible ; in fact, wherever
in his dialogues he insists on the incorrigible blindness of the historic State, allusion to the fate of him
who tried to loose the people from their chains and
lead them to the light (*Rep.* 517 A) is made in
support of his assertion. Thus, in the *Gorgias*
(521 D ff.), it is said that the wise reformer will be
judged by the multitude, as a doctor who employs
drastic methods and orders distasteful diet would
be judged by a court of children on the accusation
of a confectioner. " My children," the prosecutor
would say, " see what great evil this man hath
done unto you, maltreating even the youngest
of you with his surgeon's knife and cautery. He

starves you, he suffocates you till you are at the last gasp, he gives you most bitter draughts, and compels you to go hungry and thirsty. How different am I who have feasted you on all manner of sweet dainties." "Would not," Plato asks, " the physician's plea that he was working for the children's good be howled down by such a bench of judges ? " Never could the Athenian citizens get beyond these children's point of view, if they put to death the one man who could heal their disorders, for, as we read in the *Politicus* (299 B ff.), they would call such a man not a physician but a star-gazer, a babbler and a sophist (all terms of reproach applied to Socrates), and would themselves assume control of his patients. If anyone should introduce new remedies not sanctioned by law and custom, he should suffer the extreme penalty. For no one in a State like Athens would be held wiser than the law, and every citizen would know what rules of political medicine the law would prescribe.

Though he knew it not, the teaching of Socrates was, in its essence, cosmopolitan. Like Stephen in the Acts of the Apostles, he had to address a world-wide message to a peculiar people. Both preachers roused the anger of their audience and met their death. Plato saw, to use Nohle's illustration, that it was hopeless to tinker a wheel here

and a wheel there in the actual State ; an entirely
new machine must be built. It was all very well
to try one remedy after another, altering old laws
and laying down fresh ones ; such action on the
part of a State which is unsound at the core is like
the habit of invalids who have recourse to drugs
and nostrums, when what they need to rid them
of their maladies is a radical change in their manner
of life (*Rep.* 425 E f.). Stephen was followed by
Paul, the apostle of the Gentiles ; Plato gave up
the attempt made by Socrates to graft the states-
manship that is based on knowledge on to the
existing constitution of Athens or any other Greek
city.

The *Crito* contains nothing that is distinctively
Platonic. The dialogue represents an Athenian
gentleman named Crito, the contemporary and
oldest friend of Socrates, as coming to visit the
condemned man in prison the day before his execution. He says that the friends of Socrates
are not only willing, but very well able to effect
his escape from prison, at no great expense and
practically no risk to themselves, if only he will
consent. He will be certain of finding a warm
welcome anywhere he likes to go outside of Athens,
and Thessaly is suggested as a suitable place, because Crito has personal friends there, who will
make much of him and maintain him in safety.

C

The rest of the dialogue is nothing but the answer " no " from Socrates, set out at length. The gist of it is that we ought under no circumstances to do wrong, or to requite evil with evil. Socrates pronounces himself convinced of this principle, and gains the assent of Crito to it. " Very well then," says Socrates, " if I escaped, the laws of my country would arraign me of wrong-doing, and they would be right. There is no more to say ; wherefore suffer me, Crito, to walk in the path by which God leads me." Unconditional obedience to the State is right in the eyes of Socrates. Plato holds with his master that the authority of the law must be supreme ; if the law is found to work unjustly, that is a reason for persuading the powers that be to alter it, but none for disobedience.

The question arises whether the principle of never returning evil for evil was one on which the historical Socrates took his stand, or whether Plato was the first (with the exception of Pittacus of Mitylene) to enunciate it in Greece. We have seen (p. 4) that the contrary was the usual ethical law. Not only Hesiod, but many another sage proclaimed the duty of doing good to friends and harm to foes. Plato knew very well that all Hellenic opinion was against him, as is evident from the emphatic statement in the *Gorgias* (472), where Socrates is made to say that almost every-

one, Athenian or stranger, will take the other side,
but he, though one man against the world, will
never agree that it can be well with an evil-doer.
But did the real Socrates ever hold such a view ?
Gomperz indeed thinks that it presents a sharp
contrast to the doctrine of Xenophon's Socrates,
who looks only to what is "useful" (ὠφέλιμον),
but Xenophon himself describes the philosopher
(*Mem.* I. 2. 63) as spending a blameless public and
private life, never inflicting evil on a single soul,
so that if Socrates did not propound the principle,
at any rate he ordered his goings thereby. We
may therefore, without much misgiving, maintain
that in the *Crito* Plato was content to re-affirm
Socratic injunctions.

In the *Euthyphro* an attempt is made in the true
Socratic manner to obtain a definition of holiness.
Euthyphro and Socrates meet when the latter is
going on some business connected with the accusation against him. Euthyphro remarks that he
is starting a prosecution against his father for
manslaughter. Socrates holds up his hands in
real or pretended horror. Euthyphro rejoins that
he is completely in the right, because his father
has allowed a hired labourer, who when drunk
had killed a slave, to die in chains while waiting
till instructions should be received from Athens
what to do with him. " Is it holy," asks

Socrates, "to prosecute your father?" Euthyphro has not the slightest doubt. "Then teach me holiness," Socrates replies, "that I may put my accuser to confusion, who says that I am all wrong about religious questions." Thereupon Euthyphro puts forward five successive definitions of holiness, each of which in turn is pulled to pieces by Socrates. When Socrates tries to urge him on to make a sixth definition, because he is quite certain that, if Euthyphro did not know well what holiness is, he would never have taken so desperate a step as to bring the prosecution, poor Euthyphro pleads that he is in a hurry, and Socrates pities himself for having to go away disappointed and still unable to show his accuser that, whatever may have been his errors in the past, he now has learnt what holiness is from so great an authority as Euthyphro, and is in a position to mend his ways for the future.

Thus summarised, the dialogue seems to come to nothing but a negative result. Euthyphro's definitions represent various aspects of Athenian orthodoxy, but unlike Athenians in general he allows his orthodoxy to govern his conduct, finding justification for his conduct towards his father in the treatment given to the god Cronus by his son Zeus. Clearly such conduct would shock a fifth-century Athenian, and the moral to be drawn

is that the country needs a higher faith. When
Euthyphro is at last driven, after defining holiness
as the saying and doing of what is acceptable to
the gods in prayer and sacrifice, into an admission
that this makes holiness into a kind of trade between
men and gods, he takes the ordinary standpoint
of a professional diviner, and in point of fact he
was one. The dialogue is accordingly first and
foremost a criticism of current orthodoxy. We
get the impression that a diviner, as exemplified
by Euthyphro, is a person worthy of little respect.
Hence remembering that Socrates wished to refrain
altogether from interference with the province
of divination, we may count the somewhat con-
temptuous portrait of Euthyphro as a stage in
Plato's advance beyond his master's views.

But in addition to the critical attitude taken up
in the Euthyphro, careful search will reveal traces
of more positive teaching. It is a canon, first
laid down by Bonitz, that the key to a Platonic
dialogue is to be found in anything that remains
unrefuted. Now Socrates twice asks Euthyphro
(in 13 E and 14 A) what is the fair work that the
gods do, using men as their servants, and twice
Euthyphro returns an evasive answer, being re-
proached by Socrates for his shiftiness. From
this we may infer that Plato implies holiness to
be a joint working of gods and men to attain

some "altogether fair result" (πάγκαλον ἔργον).
Beyond this point the dialogue does not go ;
but Bonitz,[1] taking into account other passages
of Plato (*Rep.* 379 B, *Tim.* 29 E) where perfect
goodness is ascribed to God, defines holiness as
" perfected morality, only in the form that
man is conscious of being by means of it the
instrument that serves the divine working." That
is to say, holiness comprehends all the virtues,
being the knowledge of God translated into action.
We must, however, be careful to note that, so far
as the *Euthyphro* goes, Plato merely points out
the unsatisfactory nature of current notions of
holiness, at the same time giving a hint in what
direction we may look for a better definition.

[1] *Platonische Studien,* p. 234.

CHAPTER V

WE now come to a point where the subject-matter of the dialogues begins to show Platonic characteristics in a more marked manner and more frequently than heretofore. It will be remembered that Socrates thought all judgement and forecasting whether any given action is good in itself and likely to be beneficial in its results, to be beyond the province of human reason, so that, if knowledge on such subjects is desired, appeal must be made to the gods, through the art of divination. Plato does away with this appeal, and in its place introduces a new science, which he calls " the knowledge of the good," to do by means of reason the work reserved by Socrates for divination. In the *Charmides* the nature of this knowledge is developed and explained at length : in the *Laches* and the *Euthydemus*, it is already presupposed. The *Euthydemus*, it may be mentioned, belongs as regards this aspect of its teaching to the dialogues under review, which we hold to come before Plato's middle period ; but the rest of its contents, its style, and its greater length seem to give it a more appropriate place in the next group.

So far as I know, Nohle was the first to point out this link between the *Charmides*, *Laches*, and *Euthydemus*, and in what follows I am but reproducing his account of " the knowledge which makes man happy " (*Charm.* 174 A).

Human action as a whole consists of a series of special arts, each one of which has an end of its own. The doctor strives to cure the patient, the ship-captain to navigate safely and without losing ground through unskilful steersmanship. The shoemaker should make good shoes, the general should annihilate the enemy, the golf-player should get round the course with the smallest possible number of strokes (when Plato wants to use a game by way of illustration he generally chooses draughts). But supposing all these arts to work with complete success, are we necessarily the nearer to securing human well-being or happiness ? Suppose, as Plato does in the *Gorgias* (511 C ff.), that a sea-captain brings a passenger to Athens from a distant port, say in Egypt or on the Black Sea—a long voyage for those days. He will have done his professional work well, but if the passenger is afflicted with some incurable disease, Plato thinks he is to be pitied for having escaped drowning, and the skipper's art has done him no real service.

Possibly it would be better for us to go bare-footed than to wear boots, and it is at least arguable that the world would be a better place without war. A doctor may restore to health a malefactor whose renewed lease of life is very detrimental to his fellow-creatures ; excellence, again, in sport is sometimes attained by the sacrifice of higher qualities.

In the *Charmides* Socrates (*i.e.* Plato) dreams of a time when " every action will be done according to knowledge ; when no person will deceive us by professing to be a pilot if he is not, nor will a doctor or general or anyone else remain undetected, if he pretends to know something of which he is ignorant. In such circumstances shall we not be healthier in body than we are now, and when we run risks by going to sea or to war, shall we not be saved, and will not all our utensils, our wearing-apparel, and foot-gear, and all that we have for use and much besides, be artistically made, because we employ genuine craftsmen ? Nay, if you like, let us also agree that divination is the knowledge of the future, and that if wisdom [1] presides over it she turns away many braggarts, and gives us true seers as heralds of what is to come. Now when the human race is thus ordered, I allow that it will act and live in accordance with know-

[1] I follow Jowett in translating σωφροσύνη " wisdom " here.

ledge—for wisdom, being on guard, will not allow
ignorance to make her way in among us—but that
by acting in accordance with knowledge we shall
act well and find happiness, of this, my dear Critias,
we cannot yet be sure " (173 A ff.).

After some further lingering over this point,
Socrates presently bursts out : " You villain, you
keep on carrying me round in a circle, hiding from
me that after all it is not living in accordance with
knowledge that makes us act well and find happiness, not even if we know all the other sciences
put together, but only if we know a single one,
the knowledge of good and evil " (174 B f.).

The main subject under discussion in the *Charmides* is temperance. *More Socratico* the virtue is
soon decided to be a form of knowledge or wisdom.
It is after this point is reached that the above
enquiry into the one essential wisdom is started.
In the *Laches* the same question crops up when
courage is the subject in hand. A definition of
courage has been given as the knowledge of the
grounds of fear and confidence in war and all
other circumstances (194 E). Among other
objections to this definition (which is given by
Nicias, the soldier and statesman) Laches urges
that it makes out soothsayers to be courageous,
"for who but a soothsayer knows whether it
is better to live than to die ? " Nicias rejoins

that " a soothsayer ought only to know the signs
of what is to be, whether death or disease or loss
of property will come upon a man, or victory or
defeat, in war, or any other contest ; but which of
these things it is better for anyone to suffer or not
to suffer—in what way does it belong to a seer
more than to anybody else to decide this (195 E f.) ? "
Laches thinks that Nicias will not allow anyone
to be called courageous unless it be some god
(196 A).   Socrates then intervenes and declares
his belief that there is only one knowledge of good
and evil, in the past, present, or future, and that
courage is concerned not only with the knowledge
of the grounds of fear and confidence ($\delta\epsilon\iota\nu\hat{\omega}\nu\ \tau\epsilon\ \kappa\alpha\grave{\iota}$
$\theta\alpha\rho\rho\alpha\lambda\acute{\epsilon}\omega\nu\ \acute{\epsilon}\pi\iota\sigma\tau\acute{\eta}\mu\eta$), which belong to the future
only, but just as medicine involves the knowledge
of good and evil as regards health, irrespective of
time, so courage, like other sciences, understands
good and evil in the present and past and at any
time, as well as in the future.   Nicias agrees to
this, and accordingly is driven to the conclusion
that courage is not a part of virtue, as he said
earlier, but *all* virtue, whereupon it appears that
the whole matter needs further investigation, and
the conversation is adjourned.

The *Euthydemus* pursues the same strain.   In
the course of it Socrates decides that the youthful
Clinias ought to study philosophy, and it is agreed

that philosophy is the acquisition of knowledge. "Very well," says Socrates, "knowledge is of no good to us, unless we know how to use it. We should not be a whit better off if we could make rocks of gold, unless we knew what to do with the gold when we had got it (289 A). The hunter must give his quails to the cook or the quail-keeper, the mathematician (a species of hunter) must hand over his discoveries to the dialectician." "Yes," replies Clinias, "and a general can do nothing with the city he has taken, but must give it in charge to the statesman. What, then, is the art that knows how to use the fruits of all other arts or sciences, and makes us happy?" At last, after a chase as elusive as when "boys go lark-hunting," Socrates and Clinias fix upon the kingly art as being the one of which they are in search, the art which, "in the words of Aeschylus, sits at the helm of the state, and by steering and guiding all things, makes all useful" (291 D). Without this art, or rather knowledge, which is plainly equivalent to the knowledge of good and evil in the *Charmides* and *Laches*, all other forms of knowledge are unavailing.

If we ask how Plato came to this conception of the knowledge of the good as beyond and above particular branches of knowledge, it is not unreasonable to answer that he was led to it in criticising the view of divination held by Zenophon's Socrates. Let us consider *Charm.* 173 E : " You " (Critias) says Socrates, " seem to me to define the happy man "[1] " as the man who lives in accordance with some particular knowledge. And perhaps you mean him of whom I spoke just now, who knows all that is to come, the seer." To this Critias gives a qualified assent, but Socrates soon shows the seer to be as inadequate as a doctor in discerning good and evil, which is the only knowledge that really tends to man's welfare. Again, *Lach.* 196 A, as we saw above, allows a seer no more capacity than anybody else of determining whether it is better for a man to suffer or not to suffer what the seer may know is coming upon him. In the *Euthydemus* 279 D good fortune is expressly said to be wisdom : " even a child knows that." When this assertion of Socrates causes astonishment, he backs it up by declaring that the most fortunate and successful musicians, clerks, sea-captains, and doctors, are, speaking generally, those who are wise in their crafts. Hence wisdom is what makes men fortunate (*Lach.* 198 E), and the general ought to be the master, not the servant, of the soothsayer, because he knows better what is happening in war, and what is going to happen. Divination, therefore, must give place to knowledge : reason must be

---

[1] Reading ζῶντα, with Schleiermacher.

supreme in the sphere of the highest human action,
as well as in arts and crafts.

This is the great advance made by Plato in these
three dialogues. Socrates, in Xenophon, had cut
off from the domain of reason all judgement
as to what is or is not good for man; and
assigned this work to divination, that is, enquiry
of the gods through oracles and seers and omens;
Plato now extends rationalism to the whole field
of moral activity.

How the knowledge of the good is to be attained
is not indicated in any of the three dialogues. It
is of great importance to note that Laches suspects
that he who possesses it must be a god (196 A), also
that this knowledge as the kingly art ($\dot{\eta}$ $\beta\alpha\sigma\iota\lambda\iota\kappa\dot{\eta}$)
is to make men wise and good, if it is to benefit
them and render them happy (*Euthyd.* 292 C).
We shall see the force of these remarks when we
come to consider the *Republic.* Some other points
should be stored up for future use. The kingly art
is placed "at the helm of the State" (*Euthyd.*
291 D). This foreshadows the ruling or guardian
caste of the *Republic* in whom the wisdom of the
state is embodied. Further, the *Charmides* enunciates the principle of division of labour. It is said
in 171 D ff. : " If the temperate man knew *what*
he knows and what he does not know, that is to say,
if he knew that he knows the one and does *not*

know the other, it would be a great advantage to us, we say, to be temperate. For we . . . and our subjects would go through life without making mistakes. For neither should we ourselves try to do what we do not know how to do : we should seek out those who know and put it into their hands : nor should we allow our subjects to do anything except that which they could do successfully, that namely whereof they have knowledge. . . . For when error is eliminated and truth guides, men who are thus ordered must needs act rightly and well in all their doings, and those who act well must needs be happy." On this idea the *Republic* is constructed. One man, one work, is one of its chief mottoes.

CHAPTER VI

CRITICISM OF CONTEMPORARY EDUCATION

HAVING arrived at the conclusion that knowledge of the good is the knowledge that it behoves man above everything to acquire, since its possession will make him virtuous (for virtue is knowledge to Plato not less than to Socrates), Plato set to work to see what attempts were being made in his time to teach virtue. The principle that virtue is knowledge carries with it the corollary that education is the most important thing in the world, for right education will give the right knowledge, and when once the right knowledge has been gained, the will cannot fail to translate it into action, because—as we shall see more clearly shortly—the man who has attained knowledge of the good can have no motive to err, inasmuch as he knows that lapses from virtue would injure his highest interest and happiness.

Several dialogues start the question : " Can virtue be taught ? " Of these the *Protagoras* and the *Meno* deal with it directly, as their main subject. Others, such as the *Euthydemus*, keep other threads going, which though relevant to this theme, are more conspicuous. If virtue is knowledge, of course

Socrates ought to think that it can be taught.   In these dialogues, however, Socrates appears as a sceptic or enquirer on this point, who would be delighted if he could feel sure that virtue can be taught, for then his dearest hopes would be realised. What makes him doubt is the fact that nobody has been successful in teaching it.   Distinguished statesmen, who have taken the greatest pains to have their sons taught riding or music or wrestling, have signally failed in getting them taught to be good men, and surely they would not have grudged the money if the thing could be done.   Lately Socrates has been encouraged by the appearance of professors of virtue (and of everything else under the sun) who have come from distant parts to teach the youth of Athens, and he gladly welcomes every opportunity of conversing with them, so as to learn their principles and methods, but each time he comes away saddened by disenchantment, for every one of these teachers and every one of their systems turns out to be hopelessly inadequate, if not positively harmful. Plato, therefore, makes him appear to alternate between the opinion that virtue cannot be taught, but comes to men, if it ever does come, by nature and divine grace, and the conviction that it can be taught, and ought to be taught, but that all existing methods are wrong.   So far, Plato's portrait agrees with what we know of the historical Socrates,

D

though it may be doubted whether Socrates ever
subjected the whole body of sophists and rhetoricians,
who claimed to be able to supply everything needful
in the way of education, to so continuous and search-
ing a criticism as we find in the *Protagoras*, *Meno*,
Gorgias, *Phaedrus*, and *Euthydemus*. Where Plato
goes beyond his master is in the constructive side
of his teaching. He is not content to say that
contemporary systems of education are all at fault ;
he gives us in the *Republic* a detailed plan for a new
one, which, if it could be carried out in its entirety,
he thinks would ensure virtue and happiness in the
citizen and the State for evermore. As an earnest
of what might be, he started the school of the
Academy, and the effect of the impulse he then
gave has been felt increasingly ever since. The
problem of the governor is now more than ever
the problem of the educator ; but never will the
task to which the educator has to address himself
be more nobly expressed than in Plato's aspiration
to train up lovers of wisdom such that there is no
room for meanness and degrading appetites in their
souls, because they are reaching out after the whole
sum of things human and divine (*Rep.* 486 A).

The *Protagoras* is one of the liveliest of Plato's
works. Socrates relates how he had been called up
out of his bed that morning by an excited friend,
Hippocrates, with the news that Protagoras, the

famous travelling professor from the north, has just arrived in Athens. He and Hippocrates set off at once to the house where Protagoras was staying to see if he would take Hippocrates as his pupil, and on the way they had some rather disconcerting conversation as to the rashness of Hippocrates in wanting to put his soul in the keeping of somebody about whose teaching he knew next to nothing. When they reached the house they found a galaxy of talent assembled. Besides Protagoras there were present two other most celebrated sophists, Hippias and Prodicus, and a select company of men of the world, largely foreigners, whom Protagoras had collected from the cities through which he travelled, " like Orpheus charming them by his voice." All these admirers were walking up and down a cloister (built round the court-yard of the house) behind Protagoras, listening intently to his discourse, and taking the greatest care (like country-dancers) to part their lines and fall in behind whenever the great man turned in his walk. Hippias was presiding over a sort of conversation class on natural science, both he and his rival audience being seated in the opposite cloister. Meanwhile Prodicus was holding a *levée* in bed in the store-room. The capacity of the house was evidently taxed to the utmost, and the temper of the man who had opened the door to Socrates and his friend had been very much upset

by the inroad of sophists. It must have required
the self-possession of a Socrates to interrupt so highly
cultured an assembly : he regretted that he could
not hear anything more of Prodicus, who was in his
opinion "a very wise and inspired man," beyond his
deep voice booming from the inner room, but
attacking the business in hand, he went straight up
to Protagoras and introduced Hippocrates as a very
promising young man, who aspired to political
eminence, and thought that no one would help him
so well as Protagoras to attain it. Protagoras,
obviously flattered, was very gracious in his recep-
tion ; and expressed his preference for explaining
before the whole company what he could do for
Hippocrates, rather than in a private conversation.
Socrates, suspecting that he would like to show off
to his rivals his power of attracting new admirers,
proposed to call in Hippias and Prodicus to listen,
so the one was summoned from his lecturing-chair,
and the other from his bed, and the discussion
began.

Socrates starts (318 A) : "In what respect are
your pupils made better and wherein do they make
progress ?" PROTAGORAS : "In prudence ($\epsilon\vec{v}\beta o\upsilon\lambda\acute{\iota}a$)
in private and public affairs." Soc. : "Then you
profess to teach the virtue of a citizen." PROT. :
"Yes."

Then comes the ironical doubt of Socrates, referred to above (p. 49), that virtue cannot be taught, because on the one hand such distinguished people as Pericles have failed with their sons, and on the other we see that the Athenian assembly, if it wants to build docks or ships, takes expert advice from technically-trained men, and tells the police to remove any non-professional speaker, but if it is considering a question of good policy allows any body, whether carpenter, smith, rich, poor, gentle or simple, to get up and say his say, and nobody asks where he has learnt political wisdom. Plainly the world thinks it cannot be taught.

Protagoras replies with a myth, telling how when mankind were in danger of being exterminated by wild beasts, Zeus gave them justice and reverence that they might live in cities without destroying one another. At the express command of Zeus, Hermes delivered these gifts to *all* men, so that all have a share in political virtue. Moreover, if you are a bad flute-player you would be thought mad to say that you are a good one, whereas if you proclaim yourself destitute of some political virtue, say honesty, you will be thought mad for saying so, as though all men need not be good flute-players, but must possess political virtue, and be able to give counsel on matters of State.

Virtue can be taught ; otherwise, what would be the use of punishing wrong-doers ?   The State punishes them, not for revenge, but for the sake of their improvement. In point of fact, people do take trouble to get their children taught virtue, first by nurses and parents, then by schoolmasters, and then by law. If good men have bad children, it only shows that virtue is granted to different people in different degrees ; the children of good artists are often poor artists. The truth is, everybody teaches virtue according to his capabilities. " I," says Protagoras, have a special gift for teaching virtue, and therefore rightly receive large payment for my work."

So far Protagoras : then Socrates takes up the tale and cross-examines him. Protagoras very soon dislikes the process, and seizes an opportunity to deliver a showy harangue. Socrates then says that he cannot keep long discourses in his head, and must go, unless Protagoras will talk by means of short answers. The threatening storm passes away. To mollify him, Protagoras is allowed to give a kind of specimen literature lesson to Socrates, on a poem of Simonides. Socrates then gives a puzzling and very sophistical explanation of the same poem. His thesis is that sophists are mistaken in using poetry as a means of teaching virtue, because in poetry there is no knowledge, and he uses very quibbling arguments in support of it, possibly as a satire on the methods of sophists in general. Whether or no poetry can convey knowledge—a question into which we must not enter here—the point is, that Protagoras is extremely reluctant to identify virtue with knowledge. The Simonides digression over, the original discussion is resumed, and at last the unconvinced Protagoras is driven to admit—but only because he condescends thus to put an end to the persistent contentiousness of Socrates—that the particular line of argument compels him to identify virtue with knowledge (360 E).

" So then," says Socrates, " I was wrong in supposing that virtue could not be taught, for knowledge is just the thing that can be taught.   And you, Protagoras, were wrong in wanting to make out that virtue is something different from knowledge, for then it could not be taught, and yet you propose to teach it.   I should like to clear up these difficulties another time."   Protagoras agrees, with amiable compliments to Socrates for his zeal and skill in argument, saying : " I have often told my friends about you that I admire you more than anybody I meet, especially among men of your age " (Socrates was about thirty-six at the time) ; " and I declare I should not be surprised if you were to become a person celebrated for your wisdom."

The moral to be drawn by us from the dialogue is that virtue is pre-eminently a matter of education. Plato wishes to arraign the most distinguished

teachers of the day—it is not for nothing that
celebrities like Hippias and Prodicus are introduced,
as well as Protagoras—and to convince his readers
that such men are on the wrong tack, because they
have not grasped the truth that virtue is knowledge,
that is to say knowledge of the good, of which we
have caught glimpses in the *Charmides* and the
Laches. Their aim—at least the aim of some of
them—is right enough, but they do not know how
to grapple with their task. Some day Plato will
set himself to his promised work of clearing up the
difficulties, and give us the *Republic*.

It should be noted with what great respect he
speaks of Prodicus as " a very wise and inspired
man "—sophists are not all as black as they are
painted. Protagoras too, though his solemnity and
short temper obviously afford Plato much amuse-
ment, is by no means an undeserving person, in
spite of being tainted, like most other people, by a
false conceit of knowledge. He genuinely desires
to teach civil virtue and to make men good citizens,
according to his lights. Hippias is clearly not liked
by Plato, who puts a bombastic speech into his
mouth in this dialogue, and handles him rather
cruelly in the *Lesser Hippias*. He claimed to be a
walking encyclopaedia of all the learning of the day.

In the *Meno* the question " can virtue be taught ? "
is asked in the very first sentence by a young

Thessalian named Meno, who adds : " or does it come by practice or by nature, or in some other manner ? " Socrates makes the reply we should expect of him : " First we must find out what virtue is." Meno incurs the sarcasm of Socrates by giving him " a swarm " of descriptions of different virtues, instead of a definition of virtue ; as if it were an answer to the question " What is a bee ? " to describe different kinds of bees. Then Meno quotes the great sophist, Gorgias, as saying that it is the power of ruling men (73 C). Soc. : " This definition needs to be modified by the word ' justly.' " So does Meno's next attempt (77 B) : " Virtue is the power to provide for yourself good things, when you desire them : " for nobody " desires " what is bad (a truly Socratic proviso ; see above, p. 10 f. No one, if he could see far enough, would desire—βούλεσθαι —bad in preference to good, because he would be convinced that it does not pay). The definition therefore is equivalent to " the power of providing yourself with good things." There next follows a highly important section to the effect that knowledge is recollection, a doctrine which we shall more conveniently discuss hereafter.[1] In 87 C Socrates takes up the position now familiar to us that if virtue can be taught it must be knowledge, as there is nothing but knowledge that can

[1] See below, pp. 68, 81, 148.

be taught. Again, as in the Protagoras, the difficulty crops up—Where are the people who can teach it ? (89 E). Anytus, who was afterwards one of the accusers of Socrates, now arrives on the scene, and is invited, as a person of importance, to give his opinion whether sophists and their pupils are teachers and learners of virtue. Anytus repudiates their claim with vehemence : " They are manifestly the curse and destruction of those who have to do with them, and they ought to be driven out of the country by order of the state " (91 C, 92 B). He remains unmoved when told of the good reputation of Protagoras, who in the course of forty years of professional life made a fortune superior to that of the great sculptor Phidias, and was never to that day detected in corrupting his pupils ; nor is he affected by the eminence of other sophists. Anytus suggests that any Athenian gentleman (καλὸς κἀγαθός) will teach virtue better than a sophist. Socrates, of course, rejects such people, on the same grounds as in the *Protagoras*. Great men like Themistocles, Aristides, Pericles, and Thucydides have not managed to teach their sons virtue. " My friend Anytus, I am inclined to think that perhaps virtue cannot be taught." Thereupon Anytus takes offence, saying : " Socrates, I think that you are too ready to speak evil of men. If you will take my advice I should recommend you to be careful. Perhaps in any

other city it is easier to do men harm than good,
and it is certainly the case here, as I think you know
very well." With this ominous hint to Socrates of
danger to come, he disappears.

We now come to a fresh point, which will be of
great importance hereafter. Socrates casts about
to see what else virtue can be if it is not knowledge.
A person who has a true opinion of the way to a
place where he has never been, might be as good a
guide as one who really knew the way; similarly a
true opinion about virtue may be just as good a
guide to action as knowledge of virtue (97 B).
Meno is somewhat shocked at this; he rightly considers knowledge (ἐπιστήμη) to be of much higher
rank than true opinion (ὀρθὴ δόξα). Soc.: "Still,
true opinion is just as good as a working theory,
and a man who possesses it will be no less useful
than one who has knowledge. We are then agreed
that virtue is not knowledge, and not capable of
being taught. Wise men like Themistocles are wise
not by knowledge, but by rightness of opinion,
wherefore statesmen are just in the same position
towards wisdom as soothsayers and prophets; they
say many true things in an inspired frenzy, but they
know not what they say. If our investigation is
correct, virtues come neither by nature nor by
teaching, but it belongs to those who possess it
by a divine grace, without the aid of reason,

unless there be a statesman, such that he can make
others statesmen.   Such a man would be in
respect of virtue as a reality compared to shadows
(100 A)."

Thus in default of knowledge, virtue, if any be
found, seems to Plato to be based on true opinion.
If we could meet with a right education, virtue would
become knowledge.   We can imagine Plato saying
to his friends : " No system that we have already
produces virtue.   Let us try to devise a new one,
and see whether we can put it into practice in our
new school, the Academy."   It should be noted
how Socrates in the *Meno* leans towards knowledge
rather than true opinion, and only identifies virtue
with the latter because he cannot see his way to
acquiring knowledge.   It is significant that he has
a lurking doubt as to the correctness of his investigation even at the last (100 A).   Also, Meno's
reluctance to give up the notion of virtue as knowledge, which is " much more honourable than true
opinion," points to something further to come
hereafter.   So do the words : " unless there be a
statesman, such that he can make others statesmen."
When he appears, the old virtue that comes of true
opinion will give place to his wisdom, as lesser ghosts
in Hades vanished before the shade of Tiresias.

CHAPTER VII

RHETORIC AND DISPUTATION

AN important class of teachers, sometimes called sophists, has hitherto been passed over — the rhetoricians. Their claims to educate the man and the citizen must now be examined. Let us see what Gorgias, who was at the head of the profession in the fifth century B.C., says as to the effect of his art upon his pupils. Gorgias was a native of Sicily, and travelled, like Protagoras and other leading sophists, all over the Greek world. Plato chooses, as the occasion for representing an encounter between him and Socrates, a moment when Gorgias is visiting Athens for the purpose of giving lecturing displays. The conversation takes place in a large company, some of whom take a greater share than Gorgias in the discussion. Gorgias has just finished an elaborate harangue, which delighted the audience before the arrival of Socrates, and is tired, but is kindly willing to answer questions. Naturally he is asked to define his art. Like Protagoras, he is with difficulty induced to make his answers short enough to please Socrates. At last, however, rhetoric is declared to be an artificer of persuasion (πειθοῦςδ ἡμιουργός 454 A); the rhetorician is one who can persuade people even in opposition to the special expert. He will have greater power than a physician to persuade the multitude—" You mean the ignorant," interposes Socrates, "in a question of health. Then," says Socrates, " though ignorant he will appear to know among the ignorant." Gorgias assents with satisfaction; he has previously said that if an orator uses his power in order to persuade men to wrong courses, that is his fault—his skill is not to blame. Soc.: " I thought you were inconsistent when you contemplated the possibility of a rhetorician misusing his art. For you have admitted that rhetoric produces persuasion in assemblies and law-courts about the just and unjust. Therefore the rhetorician must know what is just and unjust; consequently he cannot be unjust; one who knows justice is necessarily just, and will use no skill as a weapon of unjustice."

Polus (whose name means " colt "), a young hot-headed disciple of Gorgias, cannot stand this any longer. He demands a definition from Socrates himself. Socrates calls it the semblance of part of the statesman's art (463 D). Polus: " But have not rhetoricians great power in states ? " Soc.: " They have less than any other citizen. They cannot do what they desire. Everyone desires "

($βούλεται$ as usual) " the good, rhetoricians included.
But their deeds are evil ; is it good to kill and
banish ?   Such deeds are often done unjustly
through their persuasion.   Therefore they, acting
more unjustly than others, are further than others
from doing what they really wish.   The power to kill
or burn is nought.   Anyone can assassinate a man,
or set fire to houses or ships.   But he who wreaks
unjust destruction is to be pitied, not envied."
POL. : " Surely Archelaus, the wicked tyrant of
Macedonia, is happy."   Soc. : " If he is unjust he
cannot fail to be miserable ;   though all Athens
think with you, I, one man, do not agree " (472 B,
referred to above, p. 35).   POL. : " Would you rather
be wronged than wrong another ? "   Soc. : " Yes,
and so would you."

At this point Socrates' argument takes a line that
is certainly open to question.   There is not room
here to discuss its weaknesses.   If we sympathise
with Polus in being somewhat unfairly worsted, we
are nevertheless compelled to admire humbly the
noble fearlessness of Socrates, in upholding an
ethical ideal, so far beyond the standard of his day.
We have already seen, p. 35, that there is ground for
believing that Plato here is only reinforcing his
master's precepts.   How completely he made this
maxim an essential part of his own teaching will be
still more manifest, when we come to study the

picture of the just man persecuted, in the *Republic*, Book II.

Callicles, who, as we gather from the dialogue, was a prosperous, well-educated Athenian of position, now intervenes. He thinks Socrates cannot be serious. Polus was wrong when he admitted that to wrong is more disgraceful than to be wronged (482 D). "It was this admission that caused him to be entangled by you, and if he had not been ashamed to say what he really thought, you would never have got the better of him. Convention takes this view, but nature takes the opposite side. The rule of the strong is nature's law" (we see that Callicles is a forerunner of Nietzsche) "and the ordinary code of ethics is only the endeavour of the many weak to protect themselves against the few strong. You would know this well enough, if you would only give up philosophy and do something better. Philosophy is a very pretty accomplishment for the young, but anyone who keeps on with it in later years becomes altogether ignorant of the world." Socrates wishes to know whether these strong men are required to rule themselves as well as others. Call. : "What do you mean ? " Soc. : "I mean, are they to be temperate and masters of themselves ? " Call. : "Certainly not : the more they can satisfy their appetites the better." Socrates will have none of this. He calls to mind the words of " some Sicilian or Italian of a pretty wit," who likened the souls of the intemperate to leaky sieves, for they can never be filled, and are of all the souls in Hades the most miserable. There is a fundamental disagreement between Callicles and Socrates. The one thinks unrestrained pleasure, if it be secured, is good and will produce happiness ; the other holds such a life to be the source of all misery. Even Callicles is compelled presently to admit that some pleasures are bad, and Socrates once again insists on the necessity of having a man of skill and understanding ($\tau\epsilon\chi\nu\iota\kappa\dot{o}s$ $\dot{a}\nu\acute{\eta}\rho$ 500 A) to choose between them. The rhetoric that aims simply at persuasion, without regard to the object for which persuasion is exercised, is like the cookery that seeks only the pleasure of the palate, and cares nothing for the due nourishment of the body. No rhetoric, no statesman—not even if we look at the most famous names—has yet sought to implant the virtues of justice and temperance in the people. Till that effort is made, the rhetoric of Gorgias and his fellow-teachers is in vain. The true statesman and philosopher will persuade his fellow-citizens to do what is right, by convincing them of the justness of his cause, and nothing will be more alien to him than the juggling and delusive art that goes by the name of rhetoric.

E

We said above (p. 25) that Plato seems, when he wrote the *Gorgias*, to have had a fresh outburst of bitter feeling against the city and her leaders who put his master to death. He uses harsh language against the art of rhetoric that could produce so unjust a result, and therewithal appears not to contemplate the possibility of a true art of persuasion, which shall inculcate virtue, and never be used to base ends. In the *Phaedrus*, on the other hand, together with much scorn heaped upon popular rhetoric, we are shown a splendid vision of the way in which discourse can be used to uplift the soul on mighty wings of spiritual enthusiasm. Taking as his starting-point a vapid speech of Lysias, an orator much in vogue, in praise of love, Socrates first criticises it unmercifully, then makes a kind of reply speech in a similar style of artificial oratory, as if to show that he can do better even in that department than a professional speech-maker like Lysias. Suddenly he breaks off, and launches forth into his recantation, as he calls it, for having reviled the god of love. Souls, he tells us, in a disembodied state have chariots with winged steeds whereby they can mount to the uppermost region of heaven in the train of Zeus and all the gods, who at an appointed time ride forth in winged chariots to the top of the celestial vault, there to gaze upon the region beyond the heavens, of whose glories " no earthly

poet has ever sung or will sing a worthy song."
The chariots of the gods mount easily, but those of
the human souls are hindered by a vicious steed,
who rebels against the charioteer, and refuses to
work with his yoke-fellow, a horse of noble race.
Sometimes the human soul attains to gazing on the
divine beauty and justice and truth that are only
visible to reason, "the pilot of the soul" (247 C);
more often the unruly horse only allows the
charioteer a fleeting glimpse of the region beyond
the heavens or none at all, before the wings droop
and bring both charioteer and horses down to earth.
Thereafter each soul takes the form of man, according to the degree in which it has enjoyed the vision
of the eternal realities. Those in whom the charioteer
reason has gained control over the horses will become
true philosophers, others will approach or fall away
from this, the highest lot of mortal man, in proportion to the ascendancy of the charioteer over the
spirited and appetitive elements (see p. 94) symbolised
by the good and bad horse respectively. None will
sink so low as the tyrant, in whom nought but the
vicious horse has dominion. And while incarnate in
a mortal body, if a soul sees beauty on earth, it is
forthwith filled with recollection of the divine
beauty, and unutterable longing. This is the holy
madness called love, and if the lover and his beloved
walk in the paths of wisdom, they will enslave the

part of the soul which is the abode of vice, and set free that wherein virtue dwells.

This noble rhapsody (244 A-257 B) should be read in full in order to estimate aright its claim to be a fragment of ideal rhetoric. Its splendour and enthusiasm carry the reader on with the impetus of a torrent—an impetus that is totally lacking in the two previous speeches which are carefully shaped on current rules of oratory. But it is because justice and truth are represented as the goal of love that the hymn shows what should be the aim of eloquence. When the theme is worthy, no imagery, no rhythmic harmony can be too exalted to give it due adornment. Gorgias and his fellow-teachers of rhetoric would be free from blame if they used their skill only to draw men to all things that are lovely and of good report. True rhetoric should indeed be what Gorgias called it, " an artificer of persuasion " (*Gorg.* 453 A), but persuasion is only in place when the speaker's thought is fixed on everlasting righteousness. Those rhetoricians who teach the use of subtle and ready words for base ends are as a canker eating at the heart of nations. Plato would heartily have endorsed the words of Renan (*Souvenirs de jeunesse*, p. 220) in speaking of the seminary where he received his theological training : " sans le vouloir, Saint-Sulpice, où l'on méprise la littérature, est ainsi une excellente école de style ; car la règle fondamentale du style est d'avoir uniquement en vue la pensée que l'on veut inculquer, et par conséquent d'avoir une pensée."

After the palinode in praise of love the dialogue proceeds to show that great oratory such as that of Pericles comes from philosophic training and high speculation concerning natural truths. Anyone who is a serious teacher of rhetoric will, with all the exactness in his power, study the nature of the soul, for all his striving is directed to working on the soul for good. The orator must learn the difference between man and man, and having found a fitting soul " by the help of knowledge will plant and sow in it words that are able to help themselves and him who implanted them, having in them a seed . . . which makes him who possesses it happy as far as it is possible for man " (277 A). Such an art of speaking cannot be acquired without much trouble. " And this trouble the virtuous man ought not to undertake for the sake of acting and speaking to men, but for the sake of being able to say and do with all his might what is pleasing to God " (273 E).

Hence the written is far below the spoken word in value. For a writer is constrained to set down his thoughts in a fixed manner, and cannot vary his expression in accordance with the needs and characteristics of his listeners, nor can a reader ask a writer to explain himself. Writing is to discourse as a painter's dumb images of life to living beings. The writing that is precious is the living word of knowledge inscribed on the soul of the learner. This is the seed that withers not for lack of root. If any man there be who thinks that the best of writings are but a reminder to us of the truths we learnt while our souls mounted to gaze on the divine beauty, and that the only clear and perfect way of writing is the writing on the soul concerning justice and beauty and goodness, " that man," says Socrates, " seems to be, Phaedrus, such as you and I would fain become " (278 B). If his words are based on truth, and if he is able to defend his writings by spoken arguments which make those on paper seem worthless in comparison, then we may call him more than orator or poet or statesman, we may call him —not wise, for it would be presumptuous to use a name only befitting God—but with becoming modesty, a lover of wisdom or philosopher.

Thus the result of the *Phaedrus* is in the end much the same as that of the *Gorgias*. Knowledge, or what is the same thing, virtue, is essential to the orator and the teacher of oratory. The *Gorgias* is so full of wrath against the so-called teachers and practisers of rhetoric that it loses sight of the possibility of a more excellent art of discourse. In the *Phaedrus* this omission is made good, and we are shown the outline of a training for the right exposition of noble thought which shall redound to the service of God and man. It matters little for our purpose whether we count the *Phaedrus* as earlier or later than the *Republic*. In any case it testifies to the need of a new departure in the education of Plato's fellow-citizens.

The *Euthydemus* introduces us to a new class of sophists who stand at a much lower level than Protagoras or Gorgias. Socrates tells his friend Crito that Euthydemus and Dionysodorus, who have lately come to Athens in the course of a wandering life, are made of fighting inside and out, for they are most accomplished in fighting in armour (and will teach the art for a suitable fee) and are equally skilled in the weapons of the law-court. The sophists themselves tell Socrates that their serious occupation now is to teach virtue. Socrates professes incredulity as to their power to fulfil so large a promise, but wishes them to begin immediately to instruct himself and his young companion Clinias. Then Euthydemus and Dionysodorus proceed to puzzle Clinias completely, amid shouts of laughter from the questioners and the bystanders. Socrates points out to the crestfallen Clinias, who has been driven to contradict himself in the twinkling of an eye, the quibbling character of the arguments, and asks the sophists to desist from making game of the unhappy youth. He offers to show to the best of his ability the sort of conversation-lesson that he wants to hear, and begs them to excuse his awkward efforts. As we have learnt to expect, he soon elicits from Clinias an admission that wisdom is the only good, ignorance the only evil (281 E). Therefore to get wisdom should be a man's chief endeavour, if wisdom can be taught. " What do you think about this, Clinias ? " " I think," says Clinias, " that wisdom can be taught." Socrates rejoices at this answer, and exhorts Clinias to love wisdom.

" That," continues Socrates, " is my specimen of hortatory discourse. Will you, my friends, show us how to make one in a less amateurish and more artistic manner ? " DIONYS. : " You want Clinias to become wise : therefore you want him to be what he is not, and not to be what he is—it seems then that you want him to perish." Naturally this juggle with words infuriates a member of the company. Socrates presently intervenes as a peace-maker, and desires Dionysodorus to experiment on him. As an old man who has nothing to lose, he is quite willing to be boiled in the sophists' cooking-pot, as Pelias was boiled by Medea. Dionysodorus again seizes an opportunity for an irrelevant logical puzzle, denying the possibility of contradiction. Socrates brings him back to the matter in hand, namely the search for an art which will produce wisdom, and the important confession of faith in the "kingly art" is made (291 B). This, the central point of the dialogue, we have already discussed above, p. 44. There follows an outburst of logical puzzles of the most outrageous kind, in which both sophists take part. Finally, Socrates thanks Euthydemus and Dionysodorus for their marvellous display of wisdom, but warns them that they had better henceforward unfold it only to their paying pupils, lest people should find out that it is easily learnt.

Crito, to whom Socrates describes the whole scene with the sophists, confides his anxieties about the education of his two sons, for all professional teachers of philosophy seem to him to be impossible persons, and he knows not what to do (307 A). Socrates urges him to disregard the teachers and think only of philosophy : " If she appear to be what I think her, you and yours, as the saying goes, should pursue and practise her with cheerful confidence."

We have now come to the end of the long series of dialogues, *Protagoras*, *Meno*, *Gorgias*, *Phaedrus*, and *Euthydemus*, from all of which the lesson to be learnt is the necessity of a thorough-going reform of education, in the highest interest of the individual and the state. If the absurdity of the pretensions of contentious or " eristic " sophists like Euthydemus and Dionysodorus to be educators strikes us as unworthy of serious attention, we must remember that logic in Plato's day was in its infancy. Problems of predication that seem to us mere foolishness were real difficulties, which gave deep concern to Plato himself, however much he mocks with the keenest sense of humour the acrobatic tricks of the sophists. The *Euthydemus* is well worth reading all through for its astonishingly vivid portrayal of the overwhelming banter, that is nevertheless half-serious, dealt out to bewildered hearers by the representatives of the art of disputation.

CHAPTER VIII

THE TRUE PHILOSOPHER IN LIFE AND DEATH

EARLY in the *Phaedo* (63 E f.) we meet with these words, spoken by Socrates : " Now I wish to render to you my account how it seems reasonable to me that a man who has truly spent his life in philosophy should be of good cheer when he is about to die, and that he should cherish a hope of winning the greatest good yonder, when he is dead. . . . For all who apply themselves aright to philosophy, do of themselves, unknown to the rest of men, follow nothing else except dying and death." The *Symposium* and the *Phaedo* together are an expanded discourse on this text. Gomperz is surely right, when he calls Alcibiades' speech in praise of Socrates, which is apparently an appendix to the *Symposium*, the essential root of the dialogue. " The words of Socrates," says Alcibiades (*Symp.* 221 D ff.), " are like grotesque images of Silenus which are made to open. If anyone has a mind to listen to them, they seem utterly foolish at first ; words and phrases clothe him round about, as it were the skin of a wanton satyr. For he talks of pack-asses and smiths and cobblers and tanners, and always he seems to say the same things in the same words, so that every inexperienced and unknowing man would make mock of his words. But whoso sees the images opened and finds himself within them first will discover that his words alone have sense within them, and then that they are most divine, and having in them great store of images of virtue they are of the widest comprehension, nay rather they embrace all that it behoves one who is to be good and honourable to behold."

Hitherto we have watched the development in Plato's mind of two main ideas. The first, which he took over from his master, is that lack of knowledge is the root of all evil in men and cities. The second, which presented itself more clearly to him than it did to Socrates, is the conviction that no improvement can be effected until a radically different system of training for the duties of life be introduced. Before we consider Plato's own scheme of regeneration, we pause to look at the picture he has drawn of one who has become—by the grace of God, and not thanks to those who nurtured him—a true lover of wisdom.

The earlier part of the *Symposium* need not detain us long. A banquet is taking place at the house of Agathon, the tragic poet, in honour of his success the day before in winning the prize with his first tragedy. Instead of drinking or listening to flute-playing, the company, in whom Socrates is included, agree to entertain themselves by each making a speech in praise of love. Five of those present say their say with varying degrees of eloquence and originality. Among these discourses those of Aristophanes the comic poet, and Agathon the tragedian and host, stand out, the one for its magnificent humour and vitality, the other for its polished rhetoric. As usual, we find many hits against the sophists and rhetoricians of the day, especially when Socrates declares his immense admiration for the speech of Agathon, whose peroration with its Gorgias or Gorgon-like eloquence will, he fears, turn him and his own speech into stone (198 C).

After this sally, Socrates begins in earnest, with a solemn note of criticism. " The previous speakers," he says, " have one feature in common. They have heaped upon love every kind of praise they could think of, regardless of its truth or falsehood. In my foolishness I had supposed that the praises would be true, but it seems that the proposal was that each of us should *appear* to praise love." Socrates proceeds to relate how he has been taught the true nature of love by Diotima, a wise woman from Mantinea. He, like the rest of his contemporaries had called love a mighty god, and fair, but she showed him that love is desire for what is fair and

good. A god is endowed with beauty and goodness ; love longs for the beauty and goodness he
does not yet possess, and is no god, but a spirit
mid-way between the divine and what is mortal.
He spans the gulf between God and man. He is
not wise, as a god, nor yet is he ignorant, for one
who is ignorant has no desire for wisdom, and love
is a seeker after wisdom or, to use the Greek word,
a philosopher. The lover whose longing is guided
towards true beauty will presently " consider the
beauty of the soul more precious than that of the
body . . . and " (in company with the beloved)
" will search out and bring to birth such words and
thoughts as shall improve the young, that he may
be constrained to rise yet higher and contemplate
the beautiful in institutions and in laws, and perceive that it is all of one family with itself, and so
may consider bodily beauty a trivial thing. And
after he has surveyed institutions, he will be led to
the sciences, that he may now perceive the beauty
of knowledge, and looking at last on the fulness of
beauty may no more be an unworthy trifler, no
more enslaved like a menial to beauty dwelling in
a single object . . . but facing the full sea of the
beautiful and gazing thereon, may by bountiful
philosophy become the father of many words and
thoughts full of beauty and scope sublime. And
when he has gained strength and stature here, he

will descry a single science, such as treats of the beauty I shall next describe. He who has been thus far instructed in love's mysteries, beholding things beautiful in proper sequence and after the right method, on approaching the end of his initiation will suddenly descry a wondrous beauty, even that for the sake of which all his former toils were undertaken. The beauty in the first place is ever-existent, uncreated and imperishable, knowing neither increase nor decay ; in the second place, it is not beautiful in one way and ugly in another, or beautiful at one time and ugly at another, or in one relation beautiful and in another ugly, or beautiful here and ugly there, as if beautiful in some men's eyes, and ugly in the eyes of others. . . .

" Suppose it were permitted to one to behold the beautiful itself, clear and pure and unalloyed, not tainted by human flesh or colours or any of the manifold varieties of mortal existence, but the divine beauty as it really is in its simplicity, do you think it would be an ignoble life that one should gaze thereon and ever contemplate that beauty and hold communion therewith ? Do you not rather believe that in this communion only will it be possible for a man, beholding the beautiful with the organ by which alone it can be seen, to beget, not images of virtue, but realities, for that which he embraces is not an image but the truth, and

having begotten and nourished true virtue, to
become the friend of God and attained to immortality, if ever mortal has attained ? " [1]

When this description of the heights to which a
true philosopher, whose foot is guided aright, may
strive to climb, is followed by Alcibiades' praise of
Socrates, with its insistence on his unlikeness to any
human being in the past or present, it is reasonable
to infer that Plato clothes his master's memory
with the attributes of his ideal seekers after wisdom.
If we turn to the *Phædo* the picture is completed
and the impression strengthened by contemplating
the attitude towards approaching death of one who
has " truly spent his life in philosophy."

The conversation takes place between Socrates
and a group of friends assembled in his prison on
the morning of the day at whose close he is to die.
The serenity of Socrates in the face of death causes
his friends to marvel, and is even made a matter of
reproach to him. " Why should I be troubled ? "
he replies ; " what is death, but the separation
of soul and body ? In life body is perpetually
thwarting the soul, by its appetites, by the inac-
curacy of its perceptions, or by illnesses, so that the
soul's free action is impeded. Only death effects
her deliverance. All his life the philosopher is
endeavouring to disengage himself from the body,

[1] *Symp.* 210 B-212 A, *tr.* Adam.

thereby going through, as it were, a " rehearsal of death " (μελέτη θανάτου, 81 A). " Wherefore the lover of wisdom will depart from life with joy, for he will have an assured conviction that only after death he will meet with wisdom in her purity. Would it not be the height of unreason, if such a man feared death ? "

It appears, then, that Plato expects a philosophic training to produce an ascetic detachment from life and bodily pleasures. In the *Gorgias* (493 A) he tells us, as a lesson learnt from " the wise men," that in this life we are dead, and the body is the tomb of the soul. The wise men in question were no doubt Orphic and Pythagorean teachers, who preached an austere rule of life. But it is only for the sake of a fuller and better life that the philosopher courts death. The *Symposium* has shown us how he who hungers after wisdom strives to descry eternal truth and beauty, and in the *Phaedrus* we saw that souls before birth in the body might, if blest in the highest degree, gain a fleeting vision of the ideal verities. While on earth, such souls are quickened by the sight of justice and beauty in this transitory world to a recollection (ἀνάμνησις) of the justice and beauty that never fade away, and they yearn to approach nearer to them. Death is the means by which the soul can once again quit her prison-house. If the philosopher is unmoved, nay,

F

joyous, when his hour comes, it is because he has
an overwhelming sense that his search for wisdom
in this life, highest music though it be for mortal
man (φιλοσοφία μεγίστη μουσική *Phaed.* 61 A),
is but the prelude to a song of immortality.

The proofs which Plato gives of immortality in
the *Phaedo*, *Phaedrus* and *Republic* may, for our
purposes, be passed over. What concerns us is,
not the manner in which he seeks to establish his
belief, but the belief itself. The immortality of the
soul is in Plato a cardinal dogma, forming the very
root of his philosophy. It is a vexed question
whether he held to the end of his life that the individual soul is immortal. It seems, however, fairly
clear that Plato did believe in some kind of per-
manence of individual personality even while he
taught that soul, after many wanderings, is finally
reunited with the divine mind from whence it issued.
The outstanding feature in Plato's doctrine of
immortality is his unswerving belief in pre-existence
as well as in life after death. Life, as we know it,
is the union of a soul with a body ; death is the
separation of the two factors. What, then, is the
history of a soul before it joins a particular body ?
And what after it leaves a particular body ? These
two questions are to Plato in reality one ; soul is
permanent, body is transient ; therefore soul cannot
be immortal without being pre-existent. In modern

times we are apt to think and speak only of the soul's ultimate destiny, not of its ultimate origin. We often do not regard the two questions as necessarily one, but to Plato's mind a far grander and vaster conception of immortality was present, in the thought that "the everlasting life of our soul extends backwards into the infinite past as well as forwards into the endless future." [1]

The philosopher, then, is buoyed up by the belief that he has come from a heavenly home, that while on earth he ha endeavoured to make himself like to God as far as possible (*Theaet.* 176 B) by constantly seeking after knowledge, and, finally, that after death he will in due time be again caught up and absorbed in the divine wisdom. His whole life is shaped by the thought that "man is not an earthly but a heavenly plant" (φυτὸν οὐκ ἔγγειον ἀλλὰ οὐράνιον, *Tim.* 90 A). Among men, "evils can never be destroyed, for always there must be something that is opposed to the good ; nor can they find a home among the gods, but of necessity they hover around mortal nature and this earthly place. Wherefore we must try to flee from hence thither with all speed. And flying away is to become like to God as far as possible ; and to become like him is to become just, holy and wise withal " (*Theaet.* 176 A f.).

[1] Archer-Hind, *Phaedo*, p. 9.

From the starting-point of strong and filial affection for his master, Plato has lifted the figure of Socrates on to the throne destined for the wisest, or in other words, the best, man his imagination can conceive. Such a man has within him a certain spark of divinity, for his highest faculty, the craving for wisdom, goodness and beauty, and the power to satisfy that craving so far as his mortal nature allows, links him to God. " Plato," says Mr Lewis Nettleship, " literally identifies the truly human nature in us with the divine." The question next arises : " Is it possible so to train the most gifted among mankind that their powers may be expanded to the utmost and used to guide their fellow-men in the paths of virtue and true happiness ? " We have seen how Plato cast his eye over various schemes, offered by his contemporaries for the nurture of men to take the lead in States, and found them all grievously wanting. It now becomes our task to see how he attacked the problem himself in the *Republic*.

CHAPTER IX

THE name *Republic* is a translation into English of the Latin *respublica*, Cicero's equivalent for the Greek word πολιτεία. Plato meant by it " a state," " a city," or " a commonwealth." By a kind of metaphor, the word " commonwealth " can be applied to the constitution of the individual soul in man. Plato's *Republic* seeks to depict the ideal State, and in the end he is driven to confess that such a State is nowhere to be found on earth, nor indeed is it ever likely to be. " But perhaps," he adds, " it is laid up in heaven as an ensample for him who desires to behold it, and, beholding, found a city in himself." [1] Though no society may represent the kingdom of heaven, yet a man whose soul is rightly attuned to virtue may have the kingdom of heaven within him.

The subject of the work is really the sum of human life in its ethical, political, religious and philosophic interests. More precisely, its main purpose is to discover in what way justice is better than injustice. In the first book, which is called

[1] 592 B, *tr.* Adam.

by Plato himself a prelude, after a very interesting
introductory scene, the conversation raises the
question, " What is justice ? " Two current views
of justice, with which we are already well acquainted
(see pp. 3, 64), are put forward. The first is the
convention that justice consists in doing good to
friends and ill to foes. It receives a merciless
criticism at the hands of Socrates. The second is
expounded by the blustering Thrasymachus, who,
" gathering himself up sprang at us like a wild
beast as though he would seize and carry us off "
(336 B). It is our old friend " Might is Right,"
which occupied a large portion of the *Gorgias*.
" Rulers," he says, " are stronger than the ruled.
Everywhere they pass laws in their own interest,
and what is done in their interest they call just."
According to Thucydides (I. 76, 2) this was the
principle on which Athens justified the existence of
her empire, and as it is said later on in the *Republic*
to be the theory not only of Thrasymachus but of
countless others, we may well understand here that
Plato puts it forward as an ordinary view of politics,
for which he desires to substitute a higher ideal.
Socrates proceeds to demolish the argument of
Thrasymachus by showing that every artist—and
among artists must be included rulers—aims at the
perfection of his own art. A doctor *quâ* doctor
seeks the good of his patient ; a ruler *quâ* ruler that

of his subjects. A good ruler's chief reward is escape from the misfortune of being ruled by worse men than himself. But at the end of Book I neither Thrasymachus nor Socrates is satisfied. Thrasymachus is merely unable to find answers to the arguments of Socrates, who in his turn discovers that he has been talking about justice and injustice, and their comparative advantages, without a clear notion as to what justice is.

Socrates then thought to be quit of the conversation. But Glauco, the brother of Plato, refused to let him off, saying emphatically that he has never heard anyone adequately espouse the cause of justice, and show in what way it is better than injustice (358 D). Accordingly, Glauco proposes to praise injustice at length, in order that he may afterwards hear from Socrates the refutation for which he longs of the doctrine that injustice is superior to justice. He draws the strongest possible picture of the just man, who, being thought unjust, is subjected to all manner of torture, and is finally impaled, while on the other hand an unjust man may be so skilful in his wickedness that it is never discovered, and he enjoys the highest reputation and rewards which a man can attain. Glauco is reinforced by his brother Adimantus, who brings forward argument after argument in favour of injustice, as the course more profitable to the man who can practise it with success, not only in life, but also after death, if so be that the prophets speak true, who tell of mystic atoning rites and gods who can deliver us from the consequences of wrong-doing. " Show us," finally urges Adimantus, " show us, Socrates, if you can, not merely that justice is better than injustice, but what effect each in itself has on its possessor, so that the one is a good, whether seen or unseen by gods and men, and the other an evil. No teacher has ever adequately explained how injustice is the greatest of the evils that the soul contains within herself, and justice the greatest good " (367 E and 366 E).

We now have set before us the question : " How is justice better than injustice ? " The answer to this question is the main subject of the whole dialogue. Socrates begins by doubting his competence to come to the aid of justice in distress, especially as he has not been able to convince Glauco and Adimantus by his answers to Thrasymachus. But as it is impious, while he has life and power of speech, not to come to the rescue when justice is slandered in his presence, he agrees to do what he can. And first he proposes to study justice writ large in a State, as being more easy of recognition than justice in an individual. He traces the growth of a city from its first origin in the inability of an individual to supply his own needs. From the

smallest of beginnings a community will grow till
it has within it persons qualified to practise all
useful arts, and "guardians" (φύλακες) to protect
it from invaders and, if necessary, to gain by con-
quest fresh territory for the increasing population.
Such guardians must unite in themselves two
opposite qualities, gentleness (τὸ πρᾶον) and spirit
(τὸ θυμοειδές). Noble dogs are gentle to their
friends, and fierce to those whom they do not know.
They love the known and hate the unknown ; there-
in they are true lovers of knowledge, or philosophers.
So too must our guardians be lovers of knowledge
and learning, that they may be gentle towards
their friends, and they must have spirit and swift-
ness and strength to enable them to serve their
country in war.

If, then, our State is to have such guardians, we
must set ourselves to train them from childhood
by a fitting education, and for this nothing can be
better than the time-honoured music and gymnastic. But from "music," which includes poetry
and literature generally, we must be careful to ex-
clude all such things as may be hurtful to the soul.
No tales may be admitted that impute evil and im-
morality to the gods ; nor, if we wish our guardians
to be brave, shall we allow any dread descriptions
of the life after death, or suffer poets to represent
heroes as making lamentations, or as lacking the

virtues of truth and self-control. In all arts other than literature, the arts of rhythm and melody, painting, architecture, weaving, embroidery and handicrafts (Plato hardly mentions sculpture, though he evidently would include it among the rest), if beauty of form be sought and set before the young, then will our youth " dwell in a land of health," and the spirit of music will sink into their inmost soul, endowing him who is rightly nurtured with spiritual beauty. As Plato says elsewhere (*Laws*, 653 B f.), education consists in learning to hate what ought to be hated, and to love what ought to be loved. The man who has true music in his soul will be in love with what is fairest, and the goal of music is love of the beautiful, which we have learnt from the *Symposium* (204 B) to be philosophy. The *Phaedo* (61 A) has also told us that philosophy is the highest music, and we have just seen that gentleness is a characteristic of the philosophic temperament. Therefore, gentleness of soul, the love of beauty and the love of wisdom are three inseparable results of an education that steeps the youthful mind in all things fair, and jealously wards off the taint of foulness.

So far as gymnastic, or in other words, physical training, is concerned, the main principle should be, as in the case of music, simplicity. Excess should be avoided, and hygiene should be preferred to luxurious living necessitating " cures " and medical treatment. Military training is, in Plato's opinion, the best and simplest form of physical exercise. It must be borne in mind that both music and gymnastic should be cultivated with a view to the improvement of the soul rather than of the body. Athletics undiluted produce hardness and a rough disposition ; too much music engenders softness and effeminacy. " When a man allows music to lull him and to pour into his soul through his ears as through a funnel " langorous and melancholy tunes, his spirited element is softened like glowing iron and made useful, but if he continue too far, he melts and wastes away and becomes, like Menelaus in the Iliad, a soft warrior. If, on the other hand, he works too hard at athletics and lives on a generous diet, keeping music and philosophy at arm's length, he begins by being filled with pride and spirit, and his physical courage is vastly increased ; but let him beware, for if he go too far, he will become as a wild beast, living in ignorance and ineptitude, devoid of all feeling for grace and harmony. Music and gymnastic are alike needed in due proportion to tune the philosophic and spirited elements of the soul (411 A– 412 A).

Now those who have been thus educated must be further tested in various ways, to see how far they can resist temptation. One who is proved to be a " good " guardian of himself and of the music which he has learnt, may rightly be called a guardian. The word auxiliaries may be applied to the younger men, whose probation is not ended. The utmost care must be exercised to maintain the highest possible standard in the guardian class. If a child of a humble citizen be found worthy of receiving a ruler's education, he is to have it, and become a guardian when he is ripe for the honour ; on the other hand, the children of guardians must be relegated without compunction to inferior classes, if they are found lacking in natural parts. On this the whole structure of the State depends ; that community is doomed wherein the noblest natures are shut out from power, or government is in the hands of the second and third-rate citizens.

Our State being thus founded, will be perfectly virtuous and will therefore be wise, brave, temperate and just (427 E). In what part of it shall we find wisdom ? Where, but in the knowledge possessed by the guardians, which takes counsel on behalf of the city as a whole ? From this knowledge the State gains the name of being good in counsel and truly wise, though the guardians, who alone have this, the only knowledge worthy of the name, are by a law of nature the least numerous class in the community.

Courage is evidently the peculiar characteristic of the soldier-section of the citizens, those whom we called " auxiliaries " above, holding an inter-mediate position between the true guardians and the mass of the industrial and agricultural popula-tion. Their education in music and gymnastic will have given them an indelible opinion as to what things should be feared and not feared. No solvents, such as pleasures or emotions, will destroy the fast colour of their courage, firmly fixed as it is by the habit of good order produced by the influence of right music (429 A ff., 425 A), and the strengthening element of military gymnastic (404 B).

The virtue of temperance differs from courage and wisdom in belonging to the community as a whole, being present both in rulers and in ruled, and causing the city to be a harmony of all classes. For a definition we may say that it is an agreement between those who are naturally better or worse, as to which shall rule.

Can we, then, anywhere find justice ? If we look sharply, like good huntsmen, we shall see that we have had justice before us for a long time, and have failed to recognise her. We laid down the principle that each person must do his own work, for which nature fits him. This, and this alone, is justice, the foundation of the State. If each

citizen faithfully does the task allotted to him by
nature, wisdom will grow and flourish among the
rulers, courage among rulers and auxiliaries, temperance among artisans and farmers as well as
among the two higher classes. To deal justly in
law courts is to assign to every man his own, and
to prevent aggressions on the property of others.

Thus we have discovered, what we set out on
p. 88 to find, the large letters of civic justice
in our State. We may well give it the more
general name of righteousness. Our next duty is
to seek the corresponding virtue in the individual,
using the light that we have already gained
to help us in reading the smaller characters.
The three orders in the State must be discernible
in the individual or State writ small. There is
the rational principle (τὸ λογιστικόν) that plays the
part of the guardians in the soul's commonwealth,
the spirited or courageous element (τὸ θυμοειδές)
that, rightly used, is the helper of wisdom, even
as the auxiliaries are the helpers of the rulers,
and both together should, when duly trained by
music and gymnastic, bear sway over the mass
of desires that make up the appetitive part of
soul (τὸ ἐπιθυμητικόν), welding the man into a
temperate whole, so that justice in the individual
is produced, when each faculty does its own work
in harmony with the others. When wisdom rules,

man will be at peace with himself. Justice or righteousness is the health and beauty and well-being of the soul, but vice is its disease and ugliness and weakness (444 D). Glauco thinks it is absurd any longer to enquire whether justice is better than injustice, but Socrates holds that different forms of civic and individual vice must be examined before the question is finally answered. This commonwealth that we have pictured may be called kingship or aristocracy, according to whether its rulers be one or many.

CHAPTER X

So far the development of the dialogue has pro-
ceeded in a direct line, and, as we have seen, Glauco
thinks that the discussion has really reached the
end at which it was aiming, since the company
has agreed that justice for man and State is better
than injustice. Socrates is just about to enter
on a description of inferior types of city-states,
when he is reminded that he has let fall a remark
requiring some explanation, namely, that the
principle of common property among friends should
hold good as regards wives and children (423 E f.,
449 C ff.). The remark was accepted without
question at the time, nor was there more than a
slight debate over an earlier statement by Socrates
that the guardians (including auxiliaries) must
have no private property, if they are to be truly
guardians of the whole State, and not housekeepers
or husbandmen (416 D–421 C).

The principle of community of worldly goods
we will discuss in a later chapter. At the point
we have reached, the companions of Socrates
become exercised in their minds over community

in the matter of women and children, and desire further enlightenment. Socrates reluctantly agrees to deal with a difficult subject as best he can, and launches himself as a swimmer, to use his own metaphor, making his way through three successive waves of argument. In the first wave he upholds community of education for men and women guardians (451 C–457 B); in the next community of wives and children (457 B–466 D); in the third " the greatest and most troublesome " (472 A), he enquires whether his plan of communism, and with it his ideal State, can ever come into existence. This leads him on to a far deeper investigation than any attempted earlier, regarding the nature and nurture necessary to produce perfect rulers, and it is not until Book VIII that he is able again to take up the thread where we left it at the end of the last chapter, and to depict the polities which diverge from his ideal commonwealth. The third wave of discussion, from V. 472 A to the end of VII. 541 B, forms the central and most important part of the *Republic*. It rises to unsurpassed heights of eloquence and imagination, and there is hardly a line that is not full of meaning for the metaphysician, the religious teacher, the social, political, and educational reformer in any age, not least in our own day.

To return to the first wave : Socrates maintains

G

that, in all matters concerning the administration
of a State, Nature indicates no difference between
the sexes as regards special capacities. Women
vary in their gifts and qualities, precisely as men
do. Socrates supports the traditional view that
in every physical, mental, or artistic activity women
are, on the whole, weaker than men, although, as
Glauco remarks, many women excel many men
in many things. Women, therefore, who possess
the qualities of a guardian should take their share
along with men in guiding the State, and their
training in music and gymnastics must in no way
differ from that of the male guardians. Thus
only will women reach their highest development,
and there is nothing better for a city than that
its women as well as its men should be as good as
possible (456 E).

We may congratulate ourselves on escaping the
first wave, but it is small in comparison with the
second. If mankind is to be improved by breeding,
care must be taken that the best men should unite
with the best women. The rulers are to decide what
persons are to be joined in wedlock at hymeneal
festivals, keeping their methods of procedure a secret
only known to themselves. When children are
born of good parents, they are to be reared in a
State " fold " or nursery, regarding as their parents
all those who were brides and bridegrooms at a

marriage festival a certain time before their birth. In this way the guardians will become one family, and by sharing one another's joys and sorrows, they will be bound together by community of pleasure and pain. Moreover, as they may have no private property in lands, houses, or other goods, they will be free from all quarrels occasioned by the possession of money or children or kindred (464 E). Women, then, are to share with men a common education, common responsibility for bringing up children, common guardianship of the city in peace and war. This is the natural relationship of the sexes.

At last we come to the third and mightiest wave. Is there any hope that our ideal State, where righteousness reigns supreme, and each member of each class seeks not his own, but the common good, can be approximately realised ? Nothing actual ever perfectly embodies the originator's conception, but given one change in States, no slight or easy one yet a possible departure from existing conditions, all might be well. " Until philosophers become kings in States, or those who are now called kings and sovereigns are sincere and competent lovers of wisdom, and political power becomes one with philosophy . . . there is no rest from evil for cities, my dear Glauco, nor in my judgment for the human race. Neither will this commonwealth that we have pictured in our discourse come into being, so far as may be, until that day, and see the light of the sun " (473 C f.).

This startling announcement, utterly at variance with Greek opinion of the day (see on the *Gorgias*, p. 64) is expected to provoke an immediate and violent assault on Socrates by practical politicians and others. It becomes, therefore, necessary to explain what we mean by a philosopher. We have already (see above, p. 89) defined the philosopher as one whose love of knowledge makes him gentle like a noble dog, who loves his friends. The true philosopher is he who loves, not a part of wisdom, but all wisdom, and seeks to contemplate truth (475 B and E). His vision can penetrate beyond concrete, beautiful, and just things or persons to gaze on absolute Beauty and absolute Justice. The Beautiful itself and the Just itself have true Being, and are the objects of knowledge. Those who see merely particular beautiful or just things may be said to have an opinion but not knowledge about beauty and justice. For the many beautiful and just individuals have not Being in the sense that we postulate it for absolute, eternal, and immutable Beauty and Justice. Only to those whose hearts go out to true Being can the name philosopher, lover of knowledge, lover of wisdom, rightly be applied.

Such a person will love truth with a consuming

passion, and no room will be left in his nature for covetous and sensual appetites. He will be brave, being taught by the spectacle of all time and all existence that human life is but a thing of nought. Justice and gentleness will characterise all his dealings with his fellow-men. He must be quick at learning, and apt to retain what he has learnt ; otherwise he will be void of knowledge and in the end will come to hate himself and his occupation. No self-assertion or extravagance of manner will appear in his behaviour, for the love of truth leads to due proportion in all things. Is not this the kind of man or woman to whom alone, when perfected by education and ripeness of years, we should be willing to entrust the helm of the State ?

At this point Adimantus brings forward with great force the usual arguments about the futility or roguery of so-called philosophers (see on the *Gorgias*, p. 64). Socrates admits that the reproaches are deserved. He blames partly the chaos prevailing in politics, whereby the true philosopher-statesman among politicians is like a pilot amid a crowd of mutinous sailors, who will have none of his services. A more potent cause, however, of disrepute is the fact that men profess to be philosophers who are in no way entitled to the name. Moreover, those who might in happier circumstances attain to the perfection of human wisdom and virtue are now unable to resist the corrupting influence of that clamorous monster, the mighty but ignorant populace, by whose whims they are led. Flattery on the part of interested and unscrupulous advisers completes their ruin, and the place of worthy aspirants to the hand of Philosophy is taken by base supplanters, as a little bald coppersmith who has come into some money seizes the opportunity to marry his master's daughter, when misfortune reduces her to poverty and loneliness.

A very few who cling to philosophy, take shelter as it were under a wall from the rain and wind and dust of political life, by remaining in retirement, keeping themselves unspotted from the world, so as to depart from it when the hour comes in peace and good hope, having practised the highest music all their life (see chap. viii. p. 75). This remnant have indeed done much, but their highest function is left unfulfilled, as existing commonwealths give them no proper scope for serving their fellow-citizens. It may be that in the fulness of time some ruler wise enough may appear in a country that is ready to listen to him, and then all the provisions of our ideal State may be brought about. Assuming that a perfectly just polity is not impossible, we must obviously supplement our former account of the education to be given to the rulers. That education was directed, as it were, to

setting their minds and bodies in tune, so that
nothing common or unclean should be welcome to
them. Music and gymnastics are well suited for
developing the spirited element of soul and keeping
the appetites in due subjection, but reason is the
faculty that should have control in State and individual, and such philosophers as we have in view
need a training of the intellect far more thorough
than anything yet devised. Their education must
aim at bringing them to the knowledge of the
highest Good, which from this part of the *Republic*,
and from the *Philebus* 22 C, may be identified with
the Deity, Creator, and Ruler of the Universe.[1]

Mankind in a state of ignorance are likened by
Socrates (in the famous simile of the cave at the
beginning of Book VII) to prisoners in a cave, whose
head and limbs are bound so that they only look at
the end of the cave. Behind them a fire burns, and
on the wall in front of them they see shadows of
objects borne by carriers along the breadth of the
cave. They have never seen anything else, and
have no conception of a sun-illumined world, until
a deliverer releases them from their chains, turns
them round and leads them up the toilsome path
from the cave into the light of day. This allegory
represents the task of the educator. It is his

[1] For a discussion of other views of the Platonic Supreme Good,
see Adam, *Religious Teachers of Greece*, pp. 442 ff.

business to turn the eye of the soul round so that
its gaze is directed, not to the transient things of the
visible world, but to the eternal verities which cul-
minate in the Higher Good or God.   Plato sets
forth, as the means to be adopted for this end,
a ten years' course of mathematical study (including
arithmetic, plane and solid geometry, astronomy
and harmonics, together with two years of re-
vision and co-ordination), followed by an earnest
seeking after ethical and metaphysical truth.
Dialectic is the name given to this crowning science,
since the investigation is carried on, after the
manner of Socrates, by means of question and
answer.   At different stages, both during the earlier
studies, and when dialectic is entered upon, tests
are to be applied, with a view to sifting out students
who are not competent to go through the entire
course.   When the age of thirty-five has been
reached, those students, whether men or women,
whom the long discipline has lifted out of the cave,
are to descend into it once again, and bear their
part as rulers and generals of the State, not because
they wish it themselves, but because they, being just,
will recognise the justice of this burden laid upon
them, for only in a State where rulers have open to
them a better life than ruling will those rule, who are
truly rich, not in gold, but in a life of goodness and
wisdom (521 A).   At fifty the guardians may be

released from their toil, and turn themselves to the contemplation of the Good, only renouncing their happy freedom to pursue philosophy when from time to time they take a share in the work of governing, as a necessary duty. They will train up other guardians to be like themselves, in whose hands they will leave the city when they depart to dwell in the islands of the blest.

Our third and greatest wave is now surmounted, and we have reached the conclusion that an ideal State may be possible, if philosophers worthy of the name be found, to whose hands absolute power may be trusted. Given the perfect man, he can bring about the perfect State, but it may be that he can only behold the ensample laid up in heaven, and beholding, found a city in himself. Still, "it matters not, whether it is or shall be anywhere, for the wise man (ὅ γε νοῦν ἔχων, 591 C) will do the work of that city alone, and of none other" (592 B).

CHAPTER XI

AT the beginning of Book VIII, Socrates at last enters on the discussion, postponed from the end of Book IV, of the States and corresponding individuals that fall progressively away from the perfect State and its counterpart the king-philosopher. Aristocracy, as we have seen, is the name given to the the ideal polity, in which government is in the hands of " the best," that is, the wise and virtuous. Supposing that the guardians of this State fulfil their duties imperfectly with regard to the selection of parents, the race will begin to degenerate, and dissension will arise. The spirited element will prevail over reason, so that ambition takes the place of love of righteousness. This form of government is called by Plato a " timarchy " because its ruling principle is love of honour (τιμή) and of victory. Similarly a timocratic man is one who is filled with a spirit of contention, cherishing a grudge perhaps against a philosophic father, who declines to take office in an ill-governed State, and so keeps his son out of honours and rewards. This spirit is often fostered by a querulous mother, who sees other

women taking precedence of her, and by mischief-
making old servants.

The next step downwards is to oligarchy, which
Plato represents as equivalent to plutocracy. As
the love of riches increases in a State, the love of
virtue diminishes, for " in proportion as riches and
rich men are honoured in the State, virtue and the
virtuous are dishonoured."[1] When a property qualification for rulers is established in a State, wealth
instead of knowledge determines the choice of
governors. Such communities are liable to all
sorts of evils arising from extremes of wealth and
poverty. As for the oligarchical man, he may
have had a timocratic father, who has foundered
in political life. The son takes the lesson to heart,
abjures the pursuit of honour, and devotes himself
to amassing wealth. Though his covetous impulses
are at war with his better nature, in most affairs
of life he represses them lest his possessions should
be endangered, but if he can act as a fraudulent
trustee, without fear of detection, he will.

Democracy follows oligarchy in the descending
scale. As riches increase, so does extravagance,
and men of distinction are reduced to beggary.
Such men form a class of stinging drones in the
community. The rulers profit by their financial
misfortunes and do not trouble themselves to check

[1] 551 A, *tr.* Jowett.

the evil. Then the poor discover the weakness of the rich who are set over them, and on some slight occasion they overthrow those in power, establishing a democratic government in which office is for the most part assigned by lot. This polity is " like a many-coloured garment, diversified with every shade of colour " ; [1] it is a universal provider of constitutions from which the customer who wishes to found a State can choose according to his fancy ; every man can do as seems right in his own eyes.

The following is the origin of the democratic man. An oligarchical or money-loving father is apt to keep his son too tight. The young man meets with wild associates—" tastes the honey of drones " is Plato's phrase—(559 D), and there ensues within him a contest of desires. Sometimes the more orderly desires keep the assailants in check, but if in the end the evil appetites gain the day, insolence and anarchy hold high revel in the chambers of the man's soul. One whim succeeds another ; riotous living is followed by teetotalism ; physical culture, lounging apathy, politics, philosophy, business, or soldiering, all appear by fits and starts in the life of this beautiful and many-coloured creature (561).

Last comes tyranny and the tyrannical man. Just as oligarchy was ruined by the insatiate desire

[1] 557 C, *tr.* Adam.

for wealth, so insatiate thirst for freedom produces intoxication and anarchy. Respect for rulers, parents, teachers, and elders vanishes. Even dogs and beasts of burden become self-assertive and arrogant, law and authority are set at nought. The drones in the city squeeze honey from the rich, and the workers whose means of subsistence are scanty use their political power for the robbing of hen-roosts. The people's champion is presently converted into a tyrant so soon as he tastes blood in the civil war of class against class. In the first flush of power he enacts popular measures by lavish cancelling of debts and distribution of lands. Very shortly, however, he is transformed into an oppressor, and protects himself against his growing unpopularity by a rabble body-guard of slaves and foreigners. Thus the people in shunning the frying-pan of service to free fellow-citizens have fallen into the fire of bondage to slaves. Unfettered licence has developed into tyranny.

It remains to trace the genesis of the tyrannical man. A democratic father has a son, who is drawn into a life even more lawless than the parental instability and impatience of restraint. Corresponding with the development of tyranny in the democratic city, a commanding passion will establish itself as the leader of other desires, and will finally enslave the whole man. From spendthrift he becomes criminal and parricide. In the last resort, if he finds himself in a city to match him, he will become an actual tyrant, hating and hated by all with whom he comes in contact. The real tyrant is really a slave, full of desires which he cannot gratify, a prey to fear and convulsive alarms throughout his life. The longer his rule, the worse he becomes. Friendless and wicked, he is miserable himself, and makes those about him miserable likewise.

We are now in a position to declare with a herald's voice that the kingly-philosophic man is the most virtuous and happy. The tyrannical man is the worst and most miserable, whether seen or unseen by gods and men ; the timocratic man leads a better and happier life than the oligarchical man, and he again than the democratic man. The three principles of soul—Reason, Spirit, Appetite— may be called respectively, knowledge-loving, honour-loving, gain-loving. If you ask men who embody each of these principles which of them leads the pleasantest life, each will declare for his own. Which opinion is most to be trusted ? Surely that of the lover of knowledge ; for he has within him spirit and appetite, and can reject the pleasures of ambition and gain as inferior to the sweetness of learning truth, whereas this delight is not known to those who do not possess the philosophic faculty.

Only when the spirited element and the appetites are under the due guidance of reason are such pleasures as are open to them truly attained. Man is a compound of a many-headed monster, a lion and a man.

The supporter of injustice will hardly venture to maintain his disagreement with us, when we show him that he is in effect subjecting the man to the beast within us. The upholder of justice on the contrary gives to the man, or rather to the God in man (589 D) lordship over the whole creature, taming and cherishing the gentle qualities of the many-headed monster, and curbing the wild ones. Moreover, he makes the lion his ally, and unites all the parts into one common harmonious whole. Law and education are alike directed to ensuring that the divine element shall have the upper hand, if possible by the co-operation of the individual, if not, then by the subjection of the individual to external authority. It is better for the unjust not to remain undetected, for in remedial punishment lies his best chance of deliverance from the rampant monster of his passions, and consequently of attaining peace of mind. The wise man, who has true music in him, will attune his body to the harmony of his soul ; he will not heap up riches to his own infinite harm ; he will accept such honours as he thinks will make him a better man ; and though he may dwell in a city too bad for him to serve her as a statesman, he will bear rule gladly in his own proper tate, and can at least (see above, p. 105) found an ideal city in himself.

A complete answer has now been given to Glauco's request for an exposition of the superiority of justice over injustice (358 D) in this life. The last book, after a long digression on poetry and imitative art, restores to justice the rewards, which she does receive from gods and men, though it has been shown that she can dispense with them. Plato has a robust conviction that even poverty and sickness or other adversity work together for the good of the just man in life or death, " for he is never neglected by the gods, whosoever is willing and zealous to become just, and by practising virtue to be made like to God as far as is possible for man " (613 A). The unjust man may run well in the race of life for a time, but he breaks down in the course, and justice bears away the palm. To know the rewards and punishments that are in store for righteous and unrighteous souls, we may listen to the tale of Er, the son of Armenius, who in a twelve days' trance saw the heavens opened and the recompense meted out to the souls of those who had done good and evil. This myth, showing that justice is better than injustice for the life hereafter, as well as for life on earth, finishes the defence of justice, and

Socrates concludes the dialogue in the following words : " If we follow my counsel, deeming soul immortal and able to endure all things good and all things evil, we shall ever cleave to the upward road, and follow justice together with wisdom, with all our strength ; that we may be dear both to one another and to the gods, while we abide here, and when we receive the prizes of virtue, like victors in the games, who go round gathering gifts ; and here and in the journey of a thousand years that we have described,[1] let us fare well."

[1] In the myth.

H

CHAPTER XII

THE VALUE ATTACHED BY PLATO TO EDUCATION

IT is characteristic of Plato's more important works, as Mr Archer-Hind has shown in his Introduction to the *Phaedo*, that several different subjects are interwoven in such a way that the reader can hardly say on which of them the author laid most stress. If the *Republic* is constructed so that the whole dialogue is relevant to the question, " How is justice better than injustice ? " it is very plain that education is at least one of the chief topics. We saw in chapters vi-viii the profound dissatisfaction of Plato with all contemporary education, and have now followed the principles on which he based his hopes of a complete reform. In many respects those principles have never been superseded, and, in fact, one after another of latter-day experiments in education are nothing but attempts to put various parts of Plato's theory into practice, though the source of indebtedness is often not realised.

Plato, as a disciple of Socrates, displays a hopefulness about the results of education, in which it is difficult for us to follow him, because we too often see that virtue and knowledge are by no means

114

identical in this imperfect world. Even Plato himself will not venture to say more than that in the
whole course of ages, possibly one of his philosophers
might be produced (*Rep.* 502 B). But since

> "Who aims a star shoots higher far
> Than he that means a tree,"

the loftiness itself of his ideal is an incitement to
walk as far as possible, even though our powers flag
after but a short time, along the upward road to
which he bids his hearers cleave (*Rep.* 621 C).

His conception of the problem that confronts the
educator becomes much more profound as his work
progresses. At the outset, he is concerned only to
foster the qualities of gentleness and spirit in his
guardians. Austere rhythm and melody, imagina-
tive literature that is free from all taint of vileness,
and vigorous military gymnastics are his appointed
means to this end. So far, so good, but how are
rulers to acquire the intellectual insight and spiritual
fervour necessary to true statesmen ? It is clear
that the training of reason, the master-faculty, must
be taken in hand more seriously. Mere gentleness
does not form the whole content of the philosophic
element of soul. Desire for truth is, or should be,
the characteristic passion of the philosopher, and all
those who possess the necessary natural gifts should
be helped, by wise leading, to satisfy their thirst

for knowledge, in order that those who attain wisdom may use it to uplift their fellows and order the life of the whole State aright.

The stress laid by Plato on mathematics (see p. 104) may seem to indicate an unduly narrow view of intellectual training. It cannot be denied that many of the greatest minds would starve if compelled to devote their whole attention to the study of mathematics for ten years, between the ages of twenty and thirty. It must be remembered that in Plato's day the choice of subjects was comparatively restricted, and he would be the first to accept any modifications of his curriculum that might be shown to be more efficacious in producing robustness of mind and power of exact thought. Mathematics stands to Plato for the means of strengthening the mental powers, in order that man's judgement may be made mature enough to enter on the study of the highest Good, the source of intelligence, the divine Creator of the universe.

It has been well said, in a paper lately printed for private circulation, that the terms " reason " and " rational " are used by Plato where we should speak of " spirit " and " spiritual." " There is an element of passion and ardour in Plato's ' reason ' which is very remote from our usual understanding of the term. Reason is afire with love of beauty and of goodness as well as love of truth, and so is

capable of inspiring life and action, as reason in our
ordinary sense could not inspire. To Plato the absolute reason is also the supreme good or goodness."[1]
Whether or no the system of education devised by
Plato is likely to have the effect he desired, it is to
be counted as one of his noblest conceptions, and
one most fruitful for all subsequent generations,
that those who are to serve the State should be
human beings of exceptional gifts, developed to the
utmost, and imbued with a passionate love of all
things good and beautiful.

The philosopher-statesman's duty is to produce
virtue in the State as a whole and in individuals
(*Rep.* 500 D). His own virtue, if ever he can attain
to knowledge of the Good, will rest on a basis of
truth and reason. In the *Republic* Plato seems to
look forward to this as a not impossible goal of the
highest education, even though the hint is dropped
that the ideal city is only to be found " in heaven."
Failing the true philosophic virtue founded on
knowledge, " popular and political " virtue, as the
phrase runs (*Phaed.* 82 A), founded on right opinion,
is possible for the whole community, and, even supposing the rulers have reached full knowledge of the
Good, is the only virtue attainable by the mass of
the citizens. Such virtue may come by the gift of
God (θείᾳ μοίρᾳ, *Meno* 99 E) in happily constituted

---

[1] See also Adam, *R. T. G.*, p. 329, quoted on p. 11 f. above.

persons, or it may be the result of good training in
music and gymnastics, or again, of obedience to the
behests of wise rulers (*Rep.* 590 D). It differs from
the virtue of the true philosopher, because it is
without reason (ἄνευ νοῦ) and comes by habit and
practice (ἐξ ἔθους τε καὶ μελέτης γεγονυῖα, *Phaed.*
82 B). Apparently in the *Republic* even the earlier
scheme of education in music and gymnastics is
reserved for the guardian class, including auxiliaries,
so that the artisans and tillers of the soil, apart from
instinctive impulses towards goodness, can only
contribute to the virtue of the body politic by faithfully attending to their business, according to the
rule " one man, one work," and by serving the
Divine Wisdom through keeping the laws framed by
the guardians in the image of eternal justice and
truth (*Rep.* 501 A).

The time allowed by Plato for work in the cave,
or in other words, for active direction of the community, seems very short in proportion to a man's
whole life. Fifteen years, from the age of thirty-
five to that of fifty, and occasional spells of labour
after fifty, are all that can be spared from the work
of self-education and contemplation of the Good.
Considering that the guardians have to take upon
themselves the whole task of educating their
successors as well as of administration, we must
surely suppose that Plato would have been

forced to modify his distribution of time, if he had had the chance of putting his theory into practice.

In the *Laws* Plato gives us another outline scheme of education, suited for a State where rulers and ruled are not sharply differentiated from one another as in the *Republic*. The *Laws* are the work of Plato's old age. Many scholars have not believed the book to be genuine, but besides the fact that there is a good deal of external evidence in favour of Platonic authorship, most people will refuse to believe that anyone else could have written it. The *Laws* describe the foundation and working of a commonwealth more within the reach of imperfect mankind than the city of the philosopher-kings. Virtue is to be the aim of this State, just as much as in the *Republic*, but on the one hand, the governors do not aspire to complete comprehension of God's wisdom, and on the other, education is open to all citizens. To educate is still the most important function of the State, and the work is to begin even before birth by careful treatment of the mother. In early infancy strong nurses will provide exercise by continually carrying the children about, so that their bodies may be made strong, and their souls accustomed to rhythmic motion. Babies, Plato thinks, ought to live as if they were always sailing on the sea (790 C). Music will also penetrate into the infant mind through the songs of mothers and nurses, and by the simplicity, cheerfulness and harmony of the child's surroundings, for in the earliest years all the character is most surely formed by habit (792 E). Children aged from three to six should meet at village temples— the equivalent in the *Laws* for kindergarten—under the care of chosen matrons and nurses, who will wisely check any tendency to self-will (793 E), but leave the children to find out their own amusements and occupations, for it is natural for them to do so. Plato's village-temples, if established, would have anticipated Froebel and the Dottoressa Montessori by more than two thousand years. After the age of six, boys and girls are to be taught separately in such a way that " all of them, boys and girls alike, may be sound hand and foot, and may not, if they can help, spoil the gifts of nature by bad habits."[1] To this end, both sexes should practise the handling of weapons, and also horsemanship, and the foolish custom of training only the right hand should be strongly discouraged; "people are, as it were, maimed in their hands by the folly of nurses and mothers " (794 E).

Plato's intense conservatism leads him into a certain self-contradiction, for after urging that children's sports should be spontaneous, he goes

[1] 795 D, *tr.* Jowett.

on to deprecate innovations in games, since such changes are likely to produce an unstable and revolutionary disposition in after-life. Let games, and still more, music, be designed so as to cultivate all that is best in human character, and then let them remain unchanged from generation to generation. In this respect we should follow the example of the Egyptians, who have fixed forms for music, dancing, painting and sculpture (656 D f. and 799 A). Plato is so persuaded that the best in everything can be ascertained, and is equally suitable for all conditions of society, that the danger of decay from stagnation never seems to have crossed his mind.

There are many detailed instructions in the *Laws* as to the kind of music (including literature) and physical exercise best fitted for rearing virtuous and healthy citizens. Not much is said about strict intellectual training, but arithmetic, geometry and astronomy are again advocated, and unlike the *Republic* scheme, every one is to have a taste of these subjects. Egypt is once more held up as a model, on account of its arithmetical games, where division is taught concretely by using apples and garlands for distribution among varying numbers of persons (819 B f.). A select few should study these subjects in a scientific and thorough manner, and unless a man can acquire such knowledge in addition to civic

virtues, and can see the connexion between the
sciences, music and human laws and institutions,
he is not competent to be a ruler of the whole
State, but only a subordinate to other rulers (818
A, 967 E f.).   In adult life the geography of the
country ought to be accurately learnt, for no study
is of greater importance (763 B.) ; wherefore hunting
should be encouraged as a pursuit for this and other
reasons, and it should be part of the duty of certain
officials to make a detailed exploration of the land.
The sole aim of all these provisions with regard to
education is to secure, as far as may be, a State which
is " the image of the fairest and best life " (817 B).
At the end of his life Plato clings as firmly as ever
to the doctrine that the true State should be called
the city of God, where rulers possessed of wisdom
strive to obey the principle of immortality within
us, both in public institutions and in their private
lives.   In cities where God does not rule through
human instruments " there is no refuge from evil
and trouble for the people " (713 A, E).   These
utterances exactly correspond with the declaration
in the *Republic* (see p. 99) that unless kings become
philosophers or philosophers kings, evils will never
cease in cities.   In virtue of the rational element
within him, man is not an earthly but a heavenly
plant (see above, p. 83).   Education, rightly ordered,
will fortify the godlike reason in the noblest of

mankind, and will enable them to inform the whole community with the divine spirit, through their ordinances, which the mass of the people will follow, holding a true belief in the wisdom of their rulers as servants of God.

The threefold division of classes in the *Republic* into guardians, auxiliaries, artisans and farmers, corresponding to the philosophic, spirited and appetitive elements of soul, logically allows no education to the lowest class, because only the philosophic faculty can profit by the highest training, and music and gymnastics do nothing for the appetitive element, except indirectly by teaching the superior faculties to keep it in due subjection.   In the *Laws* Plato seems to have developed a less severe view of mankind in general.   By throwing open education to all, he admits that every man may have in him some sparks of the divine, which those in authority must do their utmost to fan into a flame.

CHAPTER XIII

THE POSITION OF WOMEN IN THE PLATONIC COMMONWEALTHS

WE have spoken above (p. 120) of Plato's intense conservatism. In a sense it is true that he was utterly averse to change, but only when change in his opinion would mean degeneration from an ideal institution founded on a sure knowledge of the Good. From another point of view he was perhaps the most daring innovator that the world has ever seen. For contemporary Hellenic opinion in matters social and political he displays a complete disregard, if he thinks reform desirable, and in no part of his teaching is his antagonism to convention more marked than in his views concerning the education and duties of women.

He starts the question of women's share in the State by observing that among animals females not only bear and bring up the young, but take part in other business. The care of flocks, for instance, or hunting, is the function of dogs, irrespective of sex (*Rep.* 451 D). Why, then, should not women follow the same pursuits as men, so far as their strength allows ? But if they are to do so, they must receive the same education as men in both music and gymnastics. In this position Plato follows Socrates, and other Socratic disciples do so likewise, but Plato carries the principle that the nature of women, if weaker, is not worse than that of men to much more far-reaching consequences than any other writer of his time. He is fully aware of the ridicule that the world will pour on the notion of women going through physical and military drill along with men, " but," he pertinently remarks, " foolish is the man who identifies the laughable with anything but the bad " (452 D). The only question worthy of serious consideration is : " Are women capable of sharing the work of men ? " It was laid down as a fundamental principle of the State that every person was to do the work suited to his nature (370 B). It might therefore be argued that as women are different from men they should perform different tasks. But bald men are different from long-haired men, yet no one would forbid long-haired men to be shoemakers because bald men had taken to the trade (454 C). Individuals may have different characteristics, but these may not affect in the least aptitudes for particular pursuits. No proof is forthcoming that, because a woman bears children, she is therefore incapacitated from learning and philosophy, physical culture, music or the art of healing. In short, women may possess the qualities needed for guardian-rulers or for defenders of the country (456 A). If so, why allow these gifts to run to waste ? Women who are worthy to enter the guardian class, should be the wives and colleagues of men-guardians. It matters not that women are, in Plato's view, relatively weaker than men. The best women are only excelled by the best men, and Nature produces women whose abilities should be used to guard the city. The prevailing Hellenic custom of excluding women from all such work is contrary to nature ; there is nothing unnatural in assigning to them civic duties for which they show capacity (456 B f.).

Plato, therefore, is undaunted by any national prejudice from allowing a perfectly free and open field in all walks of life to men and women alike. All that he cares about is to find the best person to discharge a given work, and he declines to erect any artificial barriers. It is easy to see that his intellectual conviction outruns his instinct in this respect. As he develops his scheme of higher education he is plainly thinking of men-guardians only, until he sharply reminds himself (540 C.) that the fair images of philosopher-kings that he has been making represent also philosopher-queens. To be consistent, he ought also to have stated that his degenerate types of the ambitious, penurious, democratic and tyrannical man have their counterparts among women. But there was no need to insist on the defects of women in an Athenian company. The essential thing was to affirm with emphasis the principle already quoted that there is nothing better for a city than to be peopled by the best women and the best men (456 E). For this declaration women in all ages and countries owe an immense debt of gratitude to Plato.

In the *Laws* Plato is not a whit less convinced of the good that will accrue to a State through the education of women and their co-operation in public affairs. Indeed he is even more vehement in his denunciations against a policy of exclusion. If women are inferior to men, he says, in capacity for virtue, there is all the more reason for attention to their training, as neglect entails doubly serious consequences. " Wherefore the reconsideration and reform of this matter, and the ordering of all pursuits on a common footing for women as well as men, tends to further the happiness of the State " (*Laws*, 781 B). Still more vigorous are other passages. Plato has been speaking of the reported proficiency of Scythian women in horsemanship and the use of weapons, and he proceeds : " I assert that, if it is possible for these things to be, the present custom of our own country is the height of folly, in that all men and women do not with all their strength and with one accord follow the same pursuits. For by this means every city is reduced to pretty nearly half its proper size, though its taxes and burdens are the same. Yet this seems a strange error for a legislator to fall into " (805 A f.). . . . . " Let him who will, praise your legislators, but I must say what I think. The legislator ought to be whole and perfect, and not half a man only ; he ought not to let the female sex live softly and waste money and have no order of life, while he takes the utmost care of the male sex, and leaves half of life only blest with happiness, when he might have made the whole State happy." [1]

In spite, however, of this insistence on the common duties of both sexes, Plato does assign several functions to women as their special province in the work of the State. Women are expressly mentioned in the *Republic* as required to regulate, in association with men, marriages and the bringing-up of children (460 B). In the *Laws*, in addition to priestesses, who are to be elected by lot, after the age of sixty, to hold office for a year (759 D), we read of a committee of women-overseers, whose business it is to supervise married couples for the first ten years of wedlock, and report cases of obstinate misconduct to the magistrates (784 A ff.). Twelve of these women are to be in charge of the daily assemblies of young children at village temples, which we have described above, p. 120 (794 B). An army of nurses

[1] 806 C, *tr.* Jowett.

is required to care for and control the children. They will act under the authority of the women-overseers, and are, it seems, directly in the service of the State. It is the duty also of the women-overseers to decide whether young widows shall re-marry, and to arrange for the custody of children, one or both of whose parents are slaves (930 D f.). Ten of them, together with ten " guardians of the law," form a court which may allow divorce for incompatibility of temper, when their efforts at reconciliation have failed (929 E f.).

Women are thus called in as adjutants to the male officials in the State, in questions concerning the sexes and care of children, but it is clear that Plato, whenever he remembers his principles, means them, if found suitable, to take a wider share in the government and service of the country. He says : " Let the age for holding office be, in the case of a woman, forty, in that of a man, thirty years " (785 B) ; and there is no indication that by " office " he here means the special office only of a woman-overseer of marriage. Immediately after-wards he says : " Let the age of military service be, for a man, from twenty to sixty, but for a woman, if it appears needful to employ her in war, the service that is possible and fitting for each should be prescribed, after she has borne children, up to the age of fifty. Later on, we are told under

I

what circumstances a woman might be called upon
for military service. Grown-up women should
practise evolutions and tactics, because they may
have to guard the city, while the men are carrying
on operations outside, and " when enemies come
from without and compel them to fight for the
city, it is a great disgrace in a State to have its
women so shamefully trained that they are not even
willing to die and undergo any danger, like birds who
fight for their young against any of the strongest
creatures, but straightway they make a rush for the
temples and huddle at all the altars and shrines,
and cast upon the human race the imputation of
being by nature the most cowardly of all the animal
world " (814 B).

Nohle makes an interesting attempt to account
for Plato's wish to throw all public service open to
women. He assumes that Plato must have taken
this course with reluctance, and that he would have
thought the governing classes much better if they
consisted only of men. But in that case there
might be fear for the offspring of the guardians,
because the mothers would be inferior to the fathers
in education of mind and body, and future guardians
might be dragged down to the level of the industrial
class. To prevent this, wives of guardians must
be admitted into the circle of rulers. But when
there they can find nothing to do, because the com-

munistic arrangements abolish all housekeeping and separate married life, and the State takes in hand the bringing up of the children from the moment they are born. There remains no possible occupation for the women except to give them the same work as the men, in spite of their lack of qualification for it.

It seems extremely arbitrary to attribute so tortuous a mode of reasoning to Plato, in the face of his express and repeated affirmations that a State is only half a State if its women are allowed to run to waste. He sees that the work of bearing children to uphold the State in the next generation cannot possibly occupy a woman's whole life, and he rightly wishes that whatever gifts she may possess should be turned to account for the common good.

A distinguished compatriot of Dr Nohle, Dr Theodor Gomperz, in his *Greek Thinkers*,[1] while not willing to go so far as Plato in admitting women to political life, warmly praises his desire to allow them the fullest opportunity to cultivate all their faculties. Dr Gomperz thinks that if Athens of the fifth century B.C. be compared with the most civilised nations of the present day, it will be found that development is taking place in the direction recommended by Plato, and that a large part of his aims has already been accomplished.

[1] E. T. vol. iii. p. 126.

Probably Plato's half-unconscious reservation of certain duties for women foreshadows very nearly the course that events are likely to take. More and more the State busies itself with work that used to be left to private families to carry on as they pleased, and in all matters concerning the care and education of children, and the morality of the sexes, the service of women in vast numbers is already requisitioned. Nursing also, and the multitudinous agencies for promoting social welfare, though not at present mainly State employments, are publicly organised on a very large scale, and would come to grief without the labour of thousands of women. It is reasonable to expect that activities of this nature will always absorb the energies of most women who have time to spare from their own families, or whose families and households in days to come may be entirely taken charge of by public authority. But when a woman shows a special aptitude for serving her country in some other way, Plato's claim that the country will be well advised that avails itself of her power for usefulness is likely to be triumphantly vindicated in the eyes of an increasing portion of the world.

CHAPTER XIV

In the *Laws* there occurs the following passage :
" Mankind must have laws, and conform to them,
or their life would be as bad as that of the most
savage beast. And the reason of this is that no
man's nature is able to know what is best for human
society ; or knowing, always able and willing to do
what is best. In the first place, there is a difficulty
in apprehending that the true art of politics is concerned not with private but with public good (for
public good binds together States, but private only
distracts them) ; and that both the public and
private good, as well of individuals as of States, is
greater when the State and not the individual is first
considered. In the second place, although a person
knows in the abstract that this is true, yet if he be
possessed of absolute and irresponsible power, he
will never remain firm in his principles or persist in
regarding the public good as primary in the State,
and the private as secondary. . . . For if a man
were born so divinely gifted that he could naturally
apprehend the truth, he would have no need of laws
to rule over him ; for there is no law or order which

is above knowledge, nor can mind, without impiety, be deemed the subject or slave of any man, but rather the lord of all. I speak of mind, true and free, and in harmony with nature. But then there is no such mind anywhere, or at least not much ; and therefore we must choose law and order, which are second best." [1]

The aim of Plato's ideal State is public good, realised in such a way that the happiness and true self-interest of each citizen and class is promoted by contributing to the common well-being. The principle " one man, one work, in accordance with his nature," provides everybody with congenial work, " and uncongenial labour, whether above or below one's powers, is a fertile source of misery and crime." [2] Subjects have the boon of good government ; guardians escape the fate of being ruled by those worse than themselves (347 C). Nothing better than this could be wished for, but it implies that man's nature is able to know what is best for human society ; and the insight of Plato's old age noted, in the passage quoted above, the impossibility of such an aspiration.

If virtue were knowledge, and knowledge were attainable, philosophers could prescribe a walk in life to each individual that would make him contented and the whole community richly blest. Unhappily,

---

[1] 875 A ff., *tr*. Jowett.   [2] Adam on *Rep*. 415 B.

our passage from the *Laws* says "no man's nature, knowing, is always able and willing to do what is best," and again, it tells us that of the divine power to apprehend truth there is none anywhere, or at least not much, and failing this we must fall back on laws made by the best wisdom we can find among our compatriots, regulating our polity by them, instead of by the word of ideal governors.

In the *Republic*, however, a hope is cherished—though even there it sometimes seems to grow faint—of producing rulers whose knowledge of the Good imbues their characters with indelible virtue, and gives them the power of inspiring their subjects with the love of virtuous living. The State evolved under these conditions would be a society of co-workers for good, but it would depend upon the absolute rule of a body of governors whose ranks are filled up at their discretion. Guardians alone choose probationers, and have the power to reject them at several stages of their education (412 E ff., 535 A, 536 C f., 537 B, D). It is then small wonder that Plato at last comes to despair of finding persons possessed of absolute and irresponsible power, who will remain firm in their principles or persist in regarding the public good as primary in the State, and the private as secondary.

He is, in the *Republic*, already alive to the danger of degeneration in the guardians, but has devised

two safeguards, which he thinks will be adequate.
One is the reluctance of the guardians to bear office.
Those who are worthy to be true philosophers will
not willingly renounce the life of study and contemplation for labour in the cave. They will shoulder
their burden because, being just themselves, they
recognise these duties as just (520 D f.). Moreover,
only in the ideal State is the philosopher's life able
to reach perfection, and therefore it is to their highest
interest to toil in the service of that State. But
lower motives of self-interest are absent, owing to
the second guarantee against the abuse of political
power.

This safeguard consists in a thorough-going communism, applied to guardians, including auxiliaries,
but not, it seems, to the third class of citizens. No
guardian is to have any private property beyond what
is strictly necessary. Nohle remarks that the communistic principle is carried to the point of allowing
nothing to the individual but the irreducible minimum
of his personality (464 D). They are to receive a
fixed payment from the citizens, enough to meet
expenses each year and no more. They must live
in a camp and have a common mess like soldiers.
They will have no need of human gold and silver,
for they have divine riches in their souls. In
this way they will be saved themselves and will
save the city. For if they were to be allowed

homes and property they would become " house-keepers and husbandmen," instead of guardians (*Rep.* 416 D ff.).

The objection urged by Adimantus that these homeless and penniless guardians will not be happy, is brushed aside by Socrates with the significant remark : " It would not be in the least surprising if they (with the rest of the city) were most happy " (420 B), but in any case " the welfare of the city as a whole, not of any one class, is the goal to be kept in view." This goal cannot be reached unless the best citizens rule without let or hindrance. Bearing in mind the persistent tendency of mankind to misuse absolute power for the sake of personal gain, Plato devises the prohibition of private property in the case of his two ruling classes, as a safeguard against the chance of this last infirmity being found in minds nobly endowed by nature and fortified by strenuous training and many tests. The sole object of his communism, whether in goods and chattels or in domestic relationships, is to detach his guardians from material interests. Apart from this the question of collective property appears to have little interest for him. In the *Republic* he makes no express statement about the tenure of property by the mass of the citizens, but the sentence in 417 A, referred to above, prophesying the conversion of guardians into housekeepers and husbandmen, if

private possessions are allowed, seems to imply that
the non-governing class are not to be debarred from
ownership of goods. Moreover, the artisans and
husbandmen are to provide out of their earnings for
the maintenance of the rulers, so that it is clear that
they must have property which can be taxed either
in kind or money (416 E). The communistic
principle is not in itself to work salvation in the
State ; it is laid down in order to remove temptation
from the path of those who in other respects are
prepared by their nurture to walk in the ways of
righteousness and just dealing.

It appears, then, that Plato's communism, unlike
most modern socialistic theories, does not aim at
securing the material well-being of the whole
population. On the contrary, it is designed as a
check on the unrestricted power of the rulers.
Nevertheless, the more individual citizens subordinate their own interests to that of the community, the
better it is for the State. In the *Republic* Plato is
so much occupied with the creation of his ideal
guardians, that he forgets to draw in detail the
picture of the class engaged in tilling the soil. This
may be partly due, as Gomperz remarks,[1] to his
aristocratic leanings, but the *Laws* give us abundant
evidence that he was well able to take thought for
all citizens. We have already seen, pp. 119, 123,

[1] *Greek Thinkers*, E. T. iii. p. 107.

that in the *Laws* education is extended to all classes. Similarly, with regard to property, elaborate schemes are proposed to the end that destitution and excessive wealth may alike be prevented in any part of the community (739 E-745 E *et saep.*). No parent should strive to make money in order to leave great riches to his children, for the best and most harmonious (μουσικωτάτη) state of life for the young is that which is free from flattery, while not lacking the necessaries of life. " It is meet to leave to children much store of reverence, not of gold " (729 A f.). The legislator who desires to avoid antagonism, the greatest of plagues in a city, should strive that neither grievous poverty nor excessive wealth should exist among his citizens, for the evil is produced by both (744 D).

Whether the means suggested by Plato would be at all likely to achieve general well-being in either an ancient or a modern State, we cannot here stop to inquire. The permanent lesson that can be drawn from the communistic teaching in both the *Republic* and the *Laws* is the prime need of an altruistic spirit permeating society. A passage in the *Laws* sums the doctrine up with admirable fervour and clearness : " The first and highest form of the State and of the government and of the law is that in which there prevails most widely the ancient saying, that ' Friends have all things in common.' Whether there is anywhere now, or will ever be, this communion of women and children and of property, in which the private and individual is altogether banished from life, and things which are by nature private, such as eyes and ears and hands, have become common, and in some way see and hear and act in common, and all men express praise and blame and feel joy and sorrow on the same occasions, and whatever laws there are unite the city to the utmost—whether all this is possible or not, I say that no man, acting upon any other principle, will ever constitute a State which will be truer or more exalted in virtue. Whether such a State is governed by Gods or sons of Gods, one, or more than one, happy are the men, who living after this manner, dwell there ; and therefore to this we are to look for the pattern of the State, and to cling to this, and to seek with all our might for one which is like this." [1]

" Thou shalt love thy neighbour as thyself," and " Lay not up for yourselves treasures upon earth, where moth and rust doth corrupt, and where thieves break through and steal : but lay up for yourselves treasures in heaven " — these are the principles which Plato seeks to foster, by enforcing the claim of the community upon the individual, and setting at nought the importance of material

[1] 739 B ff., *tr.* Jowett.

wealth. The *Republic* draws a picture of men and women rulers devoid of ambition for self-aggrandisement and enrichment. Their desire is to lead a life of contemplation and study, and far from wishing to exercise supreme power, they only assume the direction of affairs with reluctance, because they know that the State would otherwise fall into worse hands and would no longer be a fitting abode for true philosophers.

Aristotle's criticisms of the Platonic communism in the *Politics* II. 5, though of considerable force from a practical point of view, take no account of the great distance between Plato's guardians and the level of ordinary humanity. If the ideal human virtue of which Plato dreams were possible, there would be no fear of degeneration. Even the rule forbidding private property among the guardians might safely be omitted, for, as Aristotle acutely remarks, it is not the absence of communism, but the wickedness of mankind that produces evils connected with property in existing politics (*Pol.* 1263 *b*. 23). Given truly virtuous guardians, they would spontaneously use all that they had for the benefit of the State, and communistic regulations would be superfluous.

But, as we have seen, Plato himself believes that his city is a pattern set in heaven, nowhere to be realised on earth. In the *Laws* no class is raised to so vast a height, morally and intellectually, above the rest of the community as is the body of *Republic* guardians. Consequently no class is entrusted with absolute power, and rulers are chosen by a complicated method of election from among the citizens as a whole. Laws are necessary owing to the imperfection of human nature, and among such laws Plato thinks a modified communism with regard to property will be serviceable. Any citizen who owns or acquires wealth beyond a certain maximum is to place the surplus in the hands of the State, being, as it were, subject to a super-tax of 100 per cent. (745 A). We may believe that this provision would fail to accomplish its purpose of banishing poverty from the community, but we must needs admire the spirit that animates all Plato's efforts to discourage base gain, and turn the minds of his citizens to " diviner riches."

CHAPTER XV

THE PHILOSOPHER IN THE *POLITICUS* AND
THEAETETUS. CONCLUSION

THE dialogue called *Politicus* or *Statesman* deals to a
considerable degree with the same political doctrine
as we find in the *Republic*. Older scholars, such as
Nohle, Zeller, and others have looked upon it as a
sketch preceding the more developed conception of
a State in the *Republic*, but apart from questions of
style, the non-political part of the dialogue seems
to place it in the latest group of Plato's writings,
and this view of its position is now generally held.
As in the *Republic*, the inhabitants of a State are
classified according to their functions. The lowest
class contains those who are employed in practical
and industrial arts (262, 287-290). Among them are
ranked priests and soothsayers. Next come those
who practise the arts of strategy, rhetoric and
judging (303 E ff.). All these arts are precious
and akin to the statesman's art. Still higher
are placed the administrators of a well-conducted
State, namely, those in whose souls a true and un-
shakable (μετὰ βεβαιώσεως) opinion about things
fair, just, good, and their opposites, is implanted—

implanted, that is to say, in the heaven-born element within them (309 C). Finally, there comes the Statesman himself, the good legislator, to whom alone, aided by the Muse of the kingly art, it belongs, to produce this opinion in those who have been rightly educated.

Thus the *Politicus* draws a distinction between the statesman who trains rulers, and the actual rulers who look to him for inspiration. The statesman who possesses the kingly art has knowledge, whereby he can ensure in those who carry out his teaching a true opinion concerning justice and beauty. He is, in fact, no other than the philosopher of the *Republic*, with this difference, that he does not himself descend into the cave, to take part in practical politics. He rules through his pupils, not in person. He will always be rare, for in any given city few first-rate draught-players will be found, and *a fortiori* far fewer philosopher-statesmen, since the kingly art is much more difficult than that of draught-playing (292 E).

The *Politicus* is much less sanguine than the *Republic* in tone. It recognises the difficulty of finding an adequate supply of rulers possessing knowledge, and shows how a second-best course may be adopted, where many administrators may carry out the principles of a single philosopher, who alone deserves the name of statesman. Incidentally, it may be remarked that the inferior members of the community are more like citizens of actual Greek States than those of the *Republic*. We are left to infer from the *Politicus* that the lowest class themselves form the mass of the army, and that they are only officered by members of the next higher group ; it will be remembered that the whole army of the *Republic* forms a class apart from the industrial workers. Also rhetoricians are placed, in the *Politicus*, in the same class as the leaders of the soldiers. Their business is to persuade the multitude to just action, thereby acting as helmsmen in the State, under the orders of the ruler-pilots (304 A), who determine when persuasion is to be used. No rhetoric, no power of persuasion, is needed in the *Republic*, for none but guardians have any voice in the government. Similarly, judges are unnecessary in the *Republic*, as litigation will be absent from the perfect State, but the *Politicus* includes judges in the same class as generals and rhetoricians. It seems, then, that the *Politicus* re-affirms the political teaching of the *Republic*, but at the same time makes concessions which bring the principles more within the sphere of practical politics. At one end of the scale an attempt is made to find rulers of a less exalted calibre than the philosopher-kings, whose presence in an imperfect world can but seldom be expected. On the other hand, the rank and file of

K

the community are not entirely excluded from State affairs. But, the necessity of education resting on a study of the Good remains paramount, as the only sure basis for a well-ordered State.

The *Theaetetus*, which is another of the dialogues usually held by recent scholars to belong to Plato's latest period, gives a vivid picture of the philosopher in the alien surroundings of an ordinary State. It amplifies the description in Book VI of the *Republic* of philosophers, who are not corrupted by the world, but take shelter, as it were, under a wall, by withdrawing from the storm and stress of public life (496 D). An apparently chance remark of Protagoras, one of the company, causes Socrates, in the *Theaetetus*, to contrast the philosopher with the lawyer ; the one leading a life of contemplation and leisure, the other always hurrying, speaking against time in the law-courts, stunted and servile in mind. The philosopher does not even know the way to the assembly, or the law-court. He is utterly ignorant of current events, knowing no more of them than he does of the number of pints in the sea. Yet his lack of knowledge is not affected in order to gain notoriety, but is purely due to the pre-occupation of his mind with the sum-total of things in the universe, so that, if he has to visit a law-court, he seems helpless and foolish, unable to recognise his next-door neighbour, and indifferent to all that appears great and dazzling in the eyes of the world. But let him draw the lawyer away from personal matters into discourse on the nature of justice and injustice, human happiness and misery, then it will be the lawyer's turn to grow dizzy and look foolish, knowing not how to wing his way amid heights so lofty. The only true wisdom is to flee from the evils that must needs haunt the region of earth, by becoming like to God as far as is possible to man. This is the wisdom sought by the philosopher, for the greatest penalty of evil-doing is to become like to evil (172 C-177. *Cf. Laws*, 728 B).

The philosopher of the *Theaetetus* leads a blameless life, but he misses his full growth. He can only come to his own where the environment allows him to make one among a company of spectators of all time and all existence, as in the *Republic*, or at least to pass on, as in the *Politicus*, his virtue and wisdom to disciples who cannot themselves reach the fountainhead. In all the portraits of the true philosopher that we have studied, in the *Phaedo*, the *Symposium*, the *Republic*, the *Politicus*, and the *Theaetetus*, we recognise the same essential features, the same hunger and thirst after righteousness, the same indifference to the things of this world and to life itself, and the same zeal to help mankind out of the mire of ignorance when opportunity arises.

We can now look back over the ground that we

have covered, and see how consistent, amid all its
varying manifestations, is Plato's conception of the
true good for man, whether as an individual or as
an organised community. He starts from a profound conviction that there exists an eternal Goodness, which is to be identified with an eternal Wisdom.
The human soul has kinship with this divine Wisdom,
which it has known before birth, as is shown by its
recognition of mathematical truths, to which reason
is compelled to assent even without previous teaching. "If, then," says Socrates in the *Meno*, 86 B,
"the truth about things that are always exists in
our soul, the soul will be immortal, wherefore with
a good heart you should try to seek and recollect
the knowledge that you happen not to possess at
present, or rather that you do not remember."
The sight of beauty and goodness upon earth awakes
in the soul a longing to recover the knowledge of
the heavenly Beauty and Goodness that was once
its portion (*Phaedr.* 250 ; *Symp.* 207 f.). In this life
some favoured souls are endowed with the capacity
for attaining knowledge of the everlasting Wisdom.
In the *Republic*, Books VI and VII, Plato seems to
think that such knowledge in its completest form
is not too wonderful for man, provided that the
choicest spirits are disciplined by a life-long course
of education, leading them up the steep path to the
vision of the Good. Elsewhere, recognising human

limitations, he sees that the summit is too high to reach, but he bids mankind never to weary of the endeavour to gain glimpses of the heavenly glory. The higher man can climb, the clearer will be his view. When once a true image of Goodness or Wisdom has been formed in the mind, the whole man is made virtuous.

It is the bounden duty of those who can advance the farthest towards knowledge of the Good to guide their fellow-creatures in the same road. Most are only capable of obeying in faith the precepts of their wiser teachers, but in an ideal State the humblest citizen will cheerfully carry on his appointed work, knowing that he is contributing his share towards the goodness and happiness of the whole. In existing States Plato thinks the constitution of things all awry. So far from the best men being called on to govern, every barrier is, as a rule, placed in their way to keep them out, and next to the tyranny of an unbridled and licentious potentate, a complete democracy is the worst form of State, where all citizens alike are theoretically thought competent to form equally good judgements on the needs of the nation, and even, where office, as at Athens, is held by lot, to bear rule indiscriminately.

Granted that men here and there can be trained into lovers of wisdom so zealous that their resulting

virtue is incorruptible, it will be best to leave them
to rule according to their own opinion, which will
be a true one, of what is best. If a physician is
going on a long journey, he will leave written instructions for his patients, but if he is always present,
or returns home sooner than he expected, he will
vary his treatment to suit the requirements of the
case at the moment (*Pol.* 295 C ff.). Just so it is
best that " written laws should not prevail, but a
kingly man who possesses wisdom " (*Pol.* 294 A).
But seeing that the " kingly man " is seldom or
never to be found, and that, unless his wisdom is
flawless, no man will be proof against the tempta-
tions of absolute power (*Laws*, 875), the alternative
as a second-best course is to have a code of laws,
devised with the utmost care and insight that can
be secured. Law is inevitably too rigid, and unable
to take account of the endless variations in men and
actions (*Pol.* 294 B), but, except in the perfect State,
laws there must be, and they must be enforced
" else the life of man will in no way differ from that of
the most savage beast" (*Laws*, 874 E f.). Such laws,
enacted by an inspired legislator, will preserve his
wisdom to the community as an everlasting treasure,
and will be a check on his successors, who may be
inclined to swerve from strict rectitude.

It may be observed that Plato, in his reaction
against the evils of Athenian democracy, has on his

own showing been too rigorous in excluding the mass of the population in the *Republic* from all political power and responsibility. There is hardly, except perhaps in the case of the unmitigated tyrant, a soul so perverse but that in it some glimmering of the divine fire of reason may be found. Human beings are termed philosophic, spirited, or appetitive, according to the *predominance* of one or other of these elements of soul in them, not because they exhibit one, to the exclusion of the other two. It is therefore with good reason that in the *Laws* and the *Politicus* he gives all the citizens a political part to play. An intricate method of electing rulers is described in the *Laws*, which is declared to be midway between a monarchical and democratic system, " which mean the State ought always to observe " (756 E). Since the wisdom of even the best among mankind is likely to be faulty, it is well to entrust no one ruler or aristocracy with complete power, but to use all pains in discovering candidates for office who have been trained and tested from their youth up, and to see that those who have to elect should be well versed in the spirit of the laws, so that they may have a right judgement in the selection of officials (751 C). The *Laws* provide that judges and magistrates shall have to give account of their office (761 E). In general, then, Plato's latest work is in sympathy with the aim of most modern States to

give the whole people some responsibility for the
national conduct, and to utilise the collective intelligence, while at the same time he dwells on the
importance of safeguards to prevent the vagaries of
popular judgment (*Laws* VI, *passim*).

Many provisions of the *Laws* sound strangely
modern, as for instance : " Let there be no duties
imposed in the State either on exports or on imports "
(847 B), or that children shall come to school to
learn the art of soldiery and the art of music, not
simply at the pleasure of their parents, but " education shall be compulsory on all alike, for the children
belong to the State rather than to their parents "
(804 D).   Reference has already been made to
Plato's censure of mothers and nurses who fail to
train children's left as well as their right hands
(799 E).   There are sensible remarks in 918 f. on
the keeping of hotels and shops, two occupations
held in great disrepute by fourth-century Athenians.
" These callings," says Plato, " if they were con-
ducted on principles of honest dealing, we should
honour, as we honour a mother or a nurse."

But it is not anticipations of later civilisation such
as these that give Plato's moral and political teaching a lasting value.   It is rather his insistence on
the divinity of man's soul and his fearlessness of
death—" the partnership of soul and body is in no
way better than the dissolution, as I am willing to

maintain seriously" (*Laws*, 828 D). On this principle hangs his belief in the unlimited power for good of education, and, as Plutarch says in the beginning of the *Life* of Plato's friend, Dion, his desire that "power and high place should walk hand in hand with wisdom and justice." His theory may well be summed up in words (*Laws*, 817 B) which every ruler should engrave upon his heart : "Our whole State is framed to be an imitation of the best and noblest life "—πᾶσα οὖν ἡμῖν ἡ πολιτεία συνέστηκε μίμησις τοῦ καλλίστου καὶ ἀρίστου βίου.

NOTE ON BOOKS

GREEK TEXT

THE most convenient edition is Burnet's, in the *Oxford Classical Texts*, 5 vols. The *Loeb Classical Library*, Heinemann, announces a forthcoming volume of dialogues, text and translation on opposite pages. References to Plato are made in accordance with the pages and sub-sections of the edition by Stephanus (1578). In translations the section-letters are usually omitted.

TRANSLATIONS

The Dialogues of Plato, Jowett, with analyses and introductions, 5 vols., Oxford 1892. Smaller volumes of translations are: *Trial and Death of Socrates* (*Euthyphro, Apology, Crito, Phaedo, tr.* Church); *Phaedrus, Lysis, and Protagoras, tr.* Wright; *Republic, tr.* Davies and Vaughan; all these in Macmillan's *Golden Treasury* Series. *Theaetetus and Philebus, tr.* Carlill; Swan Sonnenschein. *The Four Socratic dialogues of Plato,* (Oxford), is a smaller reprint of Jowett's version of the *Apology, Euthyphro, Crito, Phaedo.* A translation of the *Symposium* by P. B. Shelley is to be found in his *Prose Works,* or in *The Banquet and other Pieces,* Cassell's *National Library,* 1905.

OTHER WORKS

The Republic of Plato, ed. J. Adam, 2 vols., Cambridge University Press, 1902. The commentary is very full. *The Religious Teachers of Greece,* by J. Adam : T. and T. Clark, 1908. The chapters on Plato deal chiefly with Plato's mysticism, theory of education, and theory of Ideas. In my manual, " *tr.* Adam," means a translation appearing in one or other of these books.

155

Gomperz, *The Greek Thinkers*, translated from the German, in 4 vols., Murray, 1901-12, contains an account of Plato in vols. ii. and iii. Shorter manuals on Plato are *Plato* by D. G. Ritchie, T. and T. Clark, 1902 ; *Plato*, by A. E. Taylor, Constable, 1911. All these books cover the whole of Plato's philosophy.

Bosanquet's *Companion to Plato's Republic*, Rivington, 1895, and Adamson's *Education in Plato's " Republic*," Swan Sonnenschein, 1903, are very useful to students of the *Republic*. An admirable essay on *The Theory of Education in the Republic of Plato*, by R. L. Nettleship, is to be found in Abbott's *Hellenica*, Longmans, reprinted 1907. Nettleship's *Philosophical Lectures and Remains*, 2 vols., Macmillan, 1897, are invaluable.

Die Statslehre Platos, by C. Nohle, Jena, 1880, often referred to in the text, is not translated.

INDEX

THE
CAMBRIDGE MANUALS
OF SCIENCE AND LITERATURE

Published by the Cambridge University Press

GENERAL EDITORS

P. GILES, Litt.D.
Master of Emmanuel College

and

A. C. SEWARD, M.A., F.R.S.
Professor of Botany in the University of Cambridge

70 VOLUMES NOW READY

HISTORY AND ARCHAEOLOGY

Ancient Assyria. By Rev. C. H. W. Johns, Litt.D.
Ancient Babylonia. By Rev. C. H. W. Johns, Litt.D.
A History of Civilization in Palestine. By Prof. R. A. S. Macalister, M.A., F.S.A.
China and the Manchus. By Prof. H. A. Giles, LL.D.
The Civilization of Ancient Mexico. By Lewis Spence.
The Vikings. By Prof. Allen Mawer, M.A.
New Zealand. By the Hon. Sir Robert Stout, K.C.M.G., LL.D., and J. Logan Stout, LL.B. (N.Z.).
The Ground Plan of the English Parish Church. By A. Hamilton Thompson, M.A., F.S.A.
The Historical Growth of the English Parish Church. By A. Hamilton Thompson, M.A., F.S.A.
English Monasteries. By A. H. Thompson, M.A., F.S.A.
Brasses. By J. S. M. Ward, B.A., F.R.Hist.S.
Ancient Stained and Painted Glass. By F. S. Eden.

ECONOMICS

Co-partnership in Industry. By C. R. Fay, M.A.
Cash and Credit. By D. A. Barker.
The Theory of Money. By D. A. Barker.

LITERARY HISTORY

The Early Religious Poetry of the Hebrews. By the Rev.
E. G. King, D.D.

The Early Religious Poetry of Persia. By the Rev. Prof. J.
Hope Moulton, D.D., D.Theol. (Berlin).

The History of the English Bible. By John Brown, D.D.

English Dialects from the Eighth Century to the Present Day.
By W. W. Skeat, Litt.D., D.C.L., F.B.A.

King Arthur in History and Legend. By Prof. W. Lewis
Jones, M.A.

The Icelandic Sagas. By W. A. Craigie, LL.D.

Greek Tragedy. By J. T. Sheppard, M.A.

The Ballad in Literature. By T. F. Henderson.

Goethe and the Twentieth Century. By Prof. J. G. Robertson,
M.A., Ph.D.

The Troubadours. By the Rev. H. J. Chaytor, M.A.

Mysticism in English Literature. By Miss C. F. E. Spurgeon.

PHILOSOPHY AND RELIGION

The Idea of God in Early Religions. By Dr F. B. Jevons.

Comparative Religion. By Dr F. B. Jevons.

Plato : Moral and Political Ideals. By Mrs A. M. Adam.

The Moral Life and Moral Worth. By Prof. Sorley, Litt.D.

The English Puritans. By John Brown, D.D.

An Historical Account of the Rise and Development of Presby-
terianism in Scotland. By the Rt Hon. the Lord Balfour
of Burleigh, K.T., G.C.M.G.

Methodism. By Rev. H. B. Workman, D.Lit.

EDUCATION

Life in the Medieval University. By R. S. Rait, M.A.

LAW

The Administration of Justice in Criminal Matters (in England
and Wales). By G. Glover Alexander, M.A., LL.M.

BIOLOGY

The Coming of Evolution. By Prof. J. W. Judd, C.B., F.R.S.

Heredity in the Light of Recent Research. By L. Doncaster,
M.A.

Primitive Animals. By Geoffrey Smith, M.A.

The Individual in the Animal Kingdom. By J. S. Huxley, B.A.

Life in the Sea. By James Johnstone, B.Sc.

The Migration of Birds. By T. A. Coward.

BIOLOGY (continued)

Spiders. By C. Warburton, M.A.
Bees and Wasps. By O. H. Latter, M.A.
House Flies. By C. G. Hewitt, D.Sc.
Earthworms and their Allies. By F. E. Beddard, F.R.S.
The Wanderings of Animals. By H. F. Gadow, F.R.S.

ANTHROPOLOGY

The Wanderings of Peoples. By Dr A. C. Haddon, F.R.S.
Prehistoric Man. By Dr W. L. H. Duckworth.

GEOLOGY

Rocks and their Origins. By Prof. Grenville A. J. Cole.
The Work of Rain and Rivers. By T. G. Bonney, Sc.D.
The Natural History of Coal. By Dr E. A. Newell Arber.
The Natural History of Clay. By Alfred B. Searle.
The Origin of Earthquakes. By C. Davison, Sc.D., F.G.S.
Submerged Forests. By Clement Reid, F.R.S.

BOTANY

Plant-Animals: a Study in Symbiosis. By Prof. F. W. Keeble.
Plant-Life on Land. By Prof. F. O. Bower, Sc.D., F.R.S.
Links with the Past in the Plant-World. By Prof. A. C. Seward.

PHYSICS

The Earth. By Prof. J. H. Poynting, F.R.S.
The Atmosphere. By A. J. Berry, M.A.
Beyond the Atom. By John Cox, M.A.
The Physical Basis of Music. By A. Wood, M.A.

PSYCHOLOGY

An Introduction to Experimental Psychology. By Dr C. S. Myers.
The Psychology of Insanity. By Bernard Hart, M.D.

INDUSTRIAL AND MECHANICAL SCIENCE

The Modern Locomotive. By C. Edgar Allen, A.M.I.Mech.E.
The Modern Warship. By E. L. Attwood.
Aerial Locomotion. By E. H. Harper, M.A., and Allan E. Ferguson, B.Sc.
Electricity in Locomotion. By A. G. Whyte, B.Sc.
Wireless Telegraphy. By Prof. C. L. Fortescue, M.A.
The Story of a Loaf of Bread. By Prof. T. B. Wood, M.A.
Brewing. By A. Chaston Chapman, F.I.C.

SOME VOLUMES IN PREPARATION

HISTORY AND ARCHAEOLOGY

The Aryans. By Prof. M. Winternitz.
Ancient India. By Prof. E. J. Rapson, M.A.
The Peoples of India. By J. D. Anderson, M.A.
The Balkan Peoples. By J. D. Bourchier.
Canada of the present day. By C. G. Hewitt, D.Sc.
The Evolution of Japan. By Prof. J. H. Longford.
The West Indies. By Sir Daniel Morris, K.C.M.G.
The Royal Navy. By John Leyland.
Gypsies. By John Sampson.
A Grammar of Heraldry. By W. H. St John Hope, Litt.D.
Celtic Art. By Joseph Anderson, LL.D.

ECONOMICS

Women's Work. By Miss Constance Smith

LITERARY HISTORY

Early Indian Poetry. By A. A. Macdonell.
The Book. By H. G. Aldis, M.A.
Pantomime. By D. L. Murray.
Folk Song and Dance. By Miss Neal and F. Kidson.

PHYSICS

The Natural Sources of Energy. By Prof. A. H. Gibson, D.Sc.
The Sun. By Prof. R. A. Sampson.
Röntgen Rays. By Prof. W. H. Bragg, F.R.S.

BIOLOGY

The Life-story of Insects. By Prof. G. H. Carpenter.
The Flea. By H. Russell.
Pearls. By Prof. W. J. Dakin.

GEOLOGY

Soil Fertility. By E. J. Russell, D.Sc.
Coast Erosion. By Prof. T. J. Jehu.

INDUSTRIAL AND MECHANICAL SCIENCE

Coal Mining. By T. C. Cantrill.
Leather. By Prof. H. R. Procter.

www.ingramcontent.com/pod-product-compliance
Ingram Content Group UK Ltd.
Pitfield, Milton Keynes, MK11 3LW, UK
UKHW042144280225
455719UK00001B/97

9 781107 401860